ESSEX AND ITS RACE FOR THE SKIES

Graham Smith

First published 2007
© Graham Smith 2007

COUNTRYSIDE BOOKS
3 Catherine Road
Newbury, Berkshire

To view our complete range of books,
please visit us at
www.countrysidebooks.co.uk

ISBN 978 1 84674 054 1

The cover picture shows a D.H.82 Tiger Moth

Designed by Peter Davies, Nautilus Design

Produced through MRM Associates Ltd., Reading
Typeset by Mac Style, Nafferton, E. Yorkshire
Printed by Borcombe SP Ltd., Romsey

*All material for the manufacture of this book
was sourced from sustainable forests.*

CONTENTS

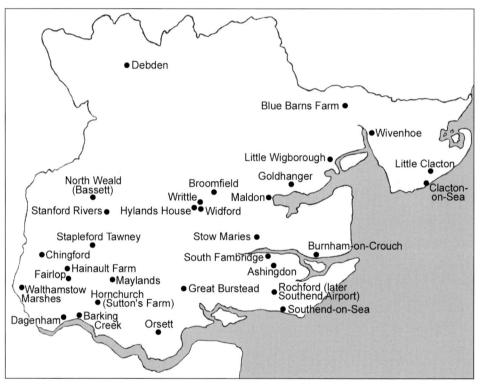

Some of the places associated with early aviation in Essex.

Introduction

After I had researched and written *Essex Airfields in the Second World War*, I was approached by various clubs and organisations to speak about the subject, and I fully realised the local thirst for knowledge of the history of flying in Essex right back to the pioneer days. In that book I was able to only outline briefly the important places, events and individuals in Essex aviation during the early decades of the twentieth century. The landing grounds at Dagenham, South Fambridge, Barking and Fairlop, along with such celebrated pioneer airmen as A.V. Roe, Frederick Handley Page, Noel Pemberton Billing and Benny Hucks, and the many brave airmen flying from Essex airfields during the First World War have all passed into aviation history; as indeed has the remarkable Edward Hillman – the 'Freddie Laker' of the thirties.

Whilst writing *Taking to the Skies: the Story of British Aviation 1903–1939*, the important part Essex played in the history of flight in this country became more apparent. I found it most difficult not to indulge the temptation to give Essex more prominence in that account.

Several aspects of the county's rich aviation heritage have appeared in publications over the years, as can be seen from my bibliography, but there is not one publication covering the whole period in detail. Therefore I felt compelled to write this history, not necessarily for publication but for my own satisfaction and enjoyment, in the hope of filling in those missing parts that I have so far been unable to expand in my existing writing and talks.

I am very pleased that Countryside Books agreed to publish my account of this long and vibrant aviation heritage and I hope that my many faithful readers will enjoy this book. I thank them for their continuing support and urging me to write a much fuller and most deserving history of Essex's 'race for the skies'; the county should be proud that it was in the forefront of such a world-changing event.

Graham Smith
Chelmsford

Chapter 1

Balloons and Airships

In December 1903 man achieved the first powered flight in a heavier-than-air flying machine and just over a century later aviation in Essex is flourishing. London Stansted Airport is one of the largest in the country and further south at Rochford is London Southend Airport. There are a number of smaller airfields around the county, which are open to private flying and air charter as well as supporting several flying and gliding clubs; two – North Weald and Rochford – can trace their origins back to the First World War. Boreham, which dates from the Second World War, is the home of the helicopters of the Essex Police and Essex Air Ambulance Service. Thus numerous aircraft, large and small along with helicopters, have become very familiar daily sights in the skies over Essex.

However, the county's aviation heritage can be traced back to the late eighteenth century when man finally achieved an ancient and cherished ambition – to escape the confines of earth and travel through the air for the first time. This was accomplished on 5th June 1783 at Annonnay in France when Joseph Montgolfier travelled about one-and-a-half miles in a hot-air balloon for a flight of ten minutes. Over the next months several other successful ascents were made in France, which was then in the forefront of ballooning. It was not until 25th August 1784 that the first manned balloon ascent took place in Great Britain, by James Tytler at Edinburgh. These successful balloon flights not only created immense public interest and excitement but they also stimulated research into flight.

The first 'aeronaut', as balloonists were then known, to land from the sky onto Essex soil, was Jean-Pierre Blanchard. In 1785 John Crosier, a Maldon miller, recorded the unique event in his diary: 'In May Mr Blanchard alighted on Laindon Hills with his balloon; he pac'd it up in a post chaise and went to London.' Blanchard, a Frenchman, had made his first balloon flight from Paris in March 1784. He came to London and in the following October began to offer 'aerial flights' from Lochee's Military Academy, Chelsea. Blanchard was probably the most famous aeronaut of the time.

Remarkably, considering the relatively few balloon flights that had been made in England then, Crosier records another landing in Essex in the following month: '3rd June, a large balloon descended in a field near Fambridge (over the Crouch some eight miles south of Maldon) with Major Money and another gentleman, both heavy men. They came down about three o'clock in the afternoon, pack'd it up and convy'd it to Maldon in a cart. The car, in the form of a boat, was superb'; an interesting use of the word 'car' to describe the balloon's carriage. With two balloon landings within the space of a couple of weeks, Essex could claim to be in the forefront of this new form of aerial transportation, albeit rather fortuitously!

The excitement continued in East Anglia that year. The aforementioned Major John Money, who lived near Norwich, was a member of a small and exclusive group of English balloon enthusiasts known as the 'Balloon Club', which included several prominent members of society. Over a month later, on 22nd July,

Major Money ascended in his balloon from Norwich and was blown out over the North Sea. His balloon finally ditched about twenty miles offshore. After almost five hours in the sea, the Major and his balloon were rescued by a Customs cutter, the *Argus* from Great Yarmouth – the first successful air/sea rescue! He became quite a celebrity as a result of a best-selling dramatic engraving by the artist Reinage. The Major was the first aeronaut to appreciate the military potential of balloons and published a treatise on the subject.

Seventeen years elapsed before the next recorded balloon landing in Essex. On 26th June 1802 one came down 'near Colchester'; the precise location is not noted. On board were Andre Garnerin and Captain R.C. Snowden. Garnerin, another Frenchman, had recently arrived in London and he had assumed the mantle of the 'most

Major John Money stranded in the North Sea – July, 1785.

celebrated aeronaut' after the death of Blanchard earlier in the year. Garnerin's ascent had been made from the Chelsea Gardens and the flight to Colchester had taken just forty-five minutes.

By this time ballooning was rapidly gaining in popularity, largely due to the enthusiastic support of wealthy members of London and provincial society. Balloon displays and exhibitions had fast become an exciting spectator sport witnessed by large crowds, especially with the added attraction of parachute descents. The leading aeronauts of the day acquired hero status.

The most famous English aeronaut of the 1820s to 1840s was Charles Green, a fruit seller from London, who had made his first ascent in 1802; by 1835 he had made over two hundred and had travelled some 6,000 miles by air in his balloon *Royal Vauxhall*. In November 1836 he accomplished a flight of 480 miles in his balloon, *Nassau*. But perhaps Green's greatest claim to fame is that he pioneered the first use of coal-gas in balloons; hitherto they had been inflated with hydrogen, a rather expensive business. Aeronauts now had a relatively cheap and convenient supply of fuel for lifting power, which had a considerable effect on the popularity of ballooning.

It was in *Nassau* that the first recorded Essex man took to the skies – George Rush, a wealthy amateur scientist and astronomer, who lived at Elsenham Hall. Rush was keen to test his improved aneroid barometer at a high altitude and he commissioned Green for the trials. Their first ascent was made on 4th September 1838 from the Vauxhall Gardens and they were accompanied by Edward Spencer, another well known aeronaut and the first member of a family destined to become famous for its aeronauts, balloons and airships. *Nassau* reached a height of 19,000 ft but this was deemed insufficient to satisfy either Rush or Green.

A second attempt was made six days later but this time without Spencer. Rush estimated that they reached a height of 27,146 ft or a little over five miles, which was then a record. The intrepid aeronauts landed safely near Lewes in Sussex; both men admitted

The perils of ballooning at high altitudes – Henry Coxwell and James Glashier had a narrow escape in the Mammoth *on 8th September 1862.*

that they had experienced 'head swellings...and bleedings from the eyes and ears...intense coldness of the feet and hands'. They had been fortunate because they were very close to the altitude where a supply of oxygen would become essential. It is not known whether Rush made another balloon ascent, although there is a record of at least one ascent from Halstead in 1848 but the names of the aeronauts have not survived.

By the 1850s the sight of balloons over Essex and their subsequent landings were no longer a novelty. Most ascended from either Vauxhall or Cremorne Gardens in London and because of the prevailing south-westerly winds many balloons were blown along in the direction of Essex, where it then became essential to land in order to avoid being carried out over the North Sea. Essex farmers had become all too familiar with balloons descending on their land damaging hedges, crops being trampled upon and their livestock frightened. In 1853 farmers in 'the parishes of East Ham, Plaistow, Leyton, Wanstead and Ilford' issued a printed proclamation under the heading 'Balloon Descents', wherein they threatened 'Aeronauts and others' with penalties for trespass on their land!

The sport showed no signs of waning in popularity despite the fact that the aeronaut was unable to control and steer the balloon whilst in flight, its direction, speed and progress being subject to the vagaries of the wind. At the same time, a number of professional and amateur engineers in the country were actively exploring the science of heavier-than-air flight and devising flying machines that could be controlled by means of an engine. On 12th January 1866 they formed an Aeronautical Society, whereby they could exchange ideas and discuss 'the science of powered flight'. Two years later the Society staged the world's first aeronautical exhibition at the Crystal Palace.

It was during the 1860s that an Essex 'birdman' was conducting his experiments into flying by the means of fabricated wings. George Faux of Chigwell Row, fitted with flapping wings, persisted in his vain attempts to fly by jumping off the roof of his house; perhaps needless to say he always quickly plummeted to earth. Faux was rather fortunate because over the centuries many 'birdmen' had fallen to their deaths in vain attempts to emulate birds. Faux claimed, 'I'm a real good flyer but I cannot alight very well.' It was only the threat of prosecution that stopped him continuing his dangerous experiments. Over the next few decades many bizarre 'ornithopters' were designed and trialled unsuccessfully; they were so called because such 'flying machines' were sustained or propelled by large flapping or oscillating wings usually powered by bicycle pedals.

Ballooning continued to hold sway and there was a flourishing Balloon Society of Great Britain. The most ardent 'balloonist' in Essex during the 1880s was Sir Claude Champion de Crespigny of Champion Lodge, Ulting near Maldon. He was a big game hunter, fearless steeplechaser and a devotee of any dangerous sport, thus 'the fascinating pursuit of ballooning' (as he described it) became his next challenge.

In June 1882 Sir Claude commissioned Joseph Simmons and his balloon to convey him across the North Sea. Simmons was a professional aeronaut who had completed hundreds of successful flights. On 10th June he brought his balloon to Maldon and placed it in a field next to the gas works. Whilst the balloon was being inflated Simmons warned Sir Claude that the wind was really 'too boisterous for a safe ascent' but Sir Claude would hear nothing of it, so enthusiastic was he to experience this new sport. During the take-off the car, or basket, careered across the field out of the control of the ground crews holding the supporting ropes. It crashed into a brick wall and in the process Sir Claude injured his leg. Nevertheless the balloon finally took to the air and less than two hours later it landed safely at Arras in France, a distance of some 170 miles; it was claimed that the English Channel had been crossed in a mere twelve minutes.

Sir Claude later wrote of 'the unspeakable splendour which so swiftly opens out to the gaze of the aerial traveller, all would admit that ballooning has great and natural attractions. The sensations the aeronaut experiences in the ascent, during his voyage through the skies, are pleasurable beyond description…'. The following year Sir Claude again contracted Simmons to attempt a flight across the North Sea. On 1st August they left from the same field at Maldon in Simmons' new balloon, *The Colonel*, and about seven hours later they landed safely at Flushing in Belgium. On his return to England the Balloon Society awarded Sir Claude its gold medal and 'a public vote of thanks'.

By a strange quirk of fate, six years later Simmons was killed in a balloon accident almost within sight of Sir Claude's residence at Ulting. On 27th August 1888 Simmons, accompanied by W.L. Field and 'Mr Miers', left the grounds of Olympia in his new balloon, *Cosmos,* bound on an ambitious long-distance flight to Vienna. *Cosmos* sailed above Romford, Brentwood, Chelmsford

A contemporary print of the fatal balloon accident at Ulting in 1888.

and Witham before Simmons considered it wise to land and anchor for the night prior to tackling the North Sea crossing. Perhaps from his previous knowledge of Ulting, Simmons attempted a landing in an open field but the balloon's grapnel became caught in some tall trees and the basket crashed to the ground with a terrific force. The three injured men were taken to Maldon for medical treatment; Simmons had fractured his skull as well as suffering severe internal injuries and he died later that evening. He was one of the last aeronauts to be killed in this dangerous pursuit.

Nevertheless ballooning continued to prosper, so much so that on 29th October 1901 the Aero Club was formed, which had as its objectives 'the encouragement of aerial-automobilism and ballooning as a sport...and to control the science and sport of balloons, airships and aeroplanes in Great Britain.' It introduced tests for aspiring aeronauts before issuing their coveted certificates. The club also arranged balloon races, which attracted large crowds. In February 1910 the club was granted Royal status but

The Aero Club organised many balloon meetings in the early 1900s.

five months later one of its founder members, the Hon. Charles S. Rolls, sadly became the first British aviator to be killed in an aeroplane accident.

During November 1901 Wanstead Flats was planned to be the scene of another aviation milestone, the first public demonstration of man-carrying kites by one of the most unlikely and certainly most flamboyant pioneer aviators – the American, Samuel Franklin

Samuel F. Cody brought his large box kite, Viva, *to Wanstead Flats in November 1901.*

Cody. His real name was 'Cowdrey' but he changed it to Cody, maybe to imply some family connection with the celebrated Colonel 'Buffalo Bill' Cody famed for his Wild West shows. Cody arrived in London in the late 1880s and was soon touring music halls with his own shows, notably *The Klondike Nugget*. However, his other abiding passion was flight and especially the design and manufacture of man-carrying kites.

In October 1901 he wrote to the War Office: 'I believe I possess certain secrets which would be of use to the Government in the way of kite flying...I can go up and down at will and my system of kites is absolutely steady in a medium wind or even in a tempest without any danger to the experimenter.' So convinced was Cody of the potential of his box kites that he arranged a series of public demonstrations to show the War Office their military capabilities.

On 14th November 1901 Cody brought his latest and largest kite, *Viva*, to Wanstead. It was 27 ft high and 13 ft wide and was claimed to be 'the largest in the world'. A large crowd had gathered, most attracted by Cody's fame as a showman but many no doubt had come to ridicule the 'eccentric birdman', as several newspapers had called him. After a delay of almost two hours, whilst Cody waited for 'a Favourable Breeze', 'the unruly crowd had grown impatient...and began to jeer the performers of this charade', as one reporter described the scene.

Probably as a result of the unfavourable reception Cody attempted to fly his *Viva* despite 'the lacklustre winds' but all to no avail and he announced that all further flying attempts were cancelled. He packed up his large kite and left to catcalls and shouts of 'Koko' – a famous British clown. Five days later, at Bury St Edmunds, Cody managed to reach a height of 300 ft but landed rather unceremoniously and heavily in a tree.

Quite undeterred, Cody continued his public displays and by the summer of 1902 his kiting experiments were matching his fame as a showman. In June 1904 Cody joined the Aeronautical Society and two years later he was engaged by the War Office as Chief Kite

Instructor, when he would concentrate on the development of a 'Motor Kite' and more especially a powered flying machine.

In 1903 Horatio Phillips was living at Southminster. He was a remarkable Victorian engineer and one of the most respected figures in the field of aerodynamics. Phillips had been experimenting with the theories of flight and flying machines since 1875. It was whilst he was at Southminster that he built his second multi-plane, which was based on the design of his first unmanned machine that had been built and trialled on a circular rack at Harrow back in 1893. His various multi-planes (a machine with two or more sets of wings mounted one above the other) were rather odd even when compared with the strange and complicated machines of the time. The machine comprised some two hundred tiny airfoils slatted in thirteen tandem frames, a device which somewhat resembled Venetian blinds.

The machine was powered by a small petrol engine and was trialled at St Lawrence Hill near Southminster in September 1903; Phillips claimed that he had reached heights of two to three feet for a distance of about twenty to thirty yards. In November 1972 a Mr J.J. Cant of Tillingham confirmed that Phillips had managed to get airborne as he had witnessed the flight. This was three months before the Wright brothers' historic powered flights at Kitty Hawk on 17th December. Phillips later moved to Streatham and in 1907 it was reported that he had again achieved powered flight in his fifth multi-plane by being airborne for a distance of 500 yards; neither were officially recognised as the first powered flights in Great Britain. The official view was that his machines lacked any real control and furthermore there was insufficient evidence at the time to justify the claims. Phillips died in 1926 at the age of 91.

The aspiration of all aeronauts was to devise a lighter-than-air machine that could be steered over a steady course. The first successful airship had appeared in France in 1852, built by Henri Giffard. An airship was then described as 'a lighter-than-air dirigible', in other words a powered balloon or machine that was

Horatio Phillips designed his second multi-plane at Southminster in 1903.

navigable or steerable. But it was the numerous successful machines designed and built from 1889 to 1906 by Alberto Santos-Dumont, a Brazilian living in Paris, which really popularised airships.

Up to 1909 there were at least two recorded landings of airships within Essex. In 1896 one, built by a Frenchman, Auguste E. Gaudron, left Alexandra Palace but only managed to get as far as Epping Forest where it crashed. Then on 9th December 1908 Henry and Herbert Spencer's airship, *Gamage 1,* which had been built to the order of Gamages Ltd, the large London department store, left Wandsworth Common on its trial flight with the two brothers on board. It landed safely at Bentley near Brentwood having flown some thirty-five miles. The Spencer family had originally been prominent in balloon manufacture and had operated as professional aeronauts, before turning most successfully to airships.

One of the Spencers' airships at Hurlingham.

Meanwhile, pioneer aviation in this country owes a deep debt of gratitude to Alfred Harmsworth, created Baron Northcliffe in 1905. He had founded the *Daily Mail* in 1896; its remarkable success led to the launching of the *Daily Mirror* in 1903 and five years later he acquired *The Times*. So convinced was he about the future of aviation that in 1906 he appointed

Lord Northcliffe (on the left) with Orville Wright in France.

Harry Harper to the *Daily Mail* as his special 'air correspondent' – believed to be the world's first specialist aviation reporter.

After the first successful flights, Lord Northcliffe famously claimed that the aeroplane had ensured that 'England is no longer an island'. He was also determined to make the story of the conquest of the air 'the *Mail*'s own'. Over the coming years Northcliffe became the most dedicated and strident advocate of British aviation and through his *Daily Mail*, he was the most generous financial supporter of pioneer aviation. The *Daily Mail*'s prize of £1,000 for the first aerial crossing of the English Channel, achieved by Louis Blériot in July 1909, would provide a strong incentive to countless aspiring British aviators.

Chapter 2

A Momentous Year for British Aviation (1909)

In 1908 Britain lagged far behind France in all aspects of aviation – not only in the number of aviators but also in the design and manufacture of aeroplanes and aero-engines. France, of course, had a long heritage of ballooning and more recently airships. The first flying training schools had been established there and since early 1905 a flying ground at Issy-les-Moulineaux, a suburb of Paris, had been available to aviators for flying trials; Paris justifiably claimed to be 'the aviation centre of the world'. In England, however, a mere handful of aviators were aspiring to claim the *Daily Mail*'s prize of £100 for the first airman to complete a round flight of a quarter of a mile in Great Britain.

The only large and secluded landing area suitable for flying tests was in the centre of the new motor-car racing track at Brooklands near Weybridge in Surrey; although during 1908 the two aviators then using Brooklands – Alliott V. Roe and John T.C. Moore-Brabazon – were refused permission to continue their trials by the Clerk of the Course, as he considered that such flying experiments brought disrepute to his track. It was only after Blériot's successful crossing of the English Channel in 1909 that the Brooklands Club became more amenable to pioneer aviators and their flying machines. However, during 1908 there were four projects in mind for establishing

Noel Pemberton Billing in 1917.

specific landing grounds and two would be sited in Essex – at South Fambridge and Dagenham.

The landing ground at South Fambridge was the brainchild of Noel Pemberton Billing, one of the most charismatic characters of early aviation. He was a true polymath; at various times during his eventful life he was an inventor, policeman, pioneer aviator, aeroplane designer, chauffeur, actor, editor, author, playwright, yacht dealer and Member of Parliament. Barbara Stoney's biography of him is entitled, *A Twentieth Century Maverick*, which aptly describes a most remarkable man.

He was born in January 1881 at Finchley into a comfortable upper-middle class family. After working as a clerk in the City of London he travelled and worked in South Africa. However, by 1904 he and his wife had moved to Crawley, Sussex, where the reports of the Wright brothers' flights fired his ambitions to build a flying machine. He constructed a glider and later a triangular kite, on which he launched himself from the roof of his house but without success. Four years later he moved to a cottage at Burnham-on-Crouch and it was then that he persuaded a wealthy friend to invest £150 towards the construction of an 'experimental flying machine' that he had designed, but only on the proviso that he found a suitable site for its construction and testing.

With his usual enthusiasm Pemberton Billing set about the task of finding suitable land near to Burnham and he was soon successful. About four miles west of Burnham is the somewhat remote village of South Fambridge, where there was an area of bleak flat marshland around the disused buildings of an hydraulic crane factory. The owners of the land were prepared to offer him an option on the whole area including much of the village. With a certain acumen Pemberton Billing managed to sell most of the other land for the total cost of his purchase, so he obtained this landing ground and buildings for virtually nothing. He had rather grandiose plans for the site as a place for flying machine experimenters to build and test their machines, what he later called a 'Colony of British Aerocraft'.

In February 1909 a report appeared in the *Essex Weekly News*:

At Dagenham land has already been secured by the Aero Club [sic] for trials of airships and according to other reports, another well-equipped station is likely to be established in Essex on about 3,000 acres of land near South Fambridge. In the latter project the military side of aeronautics will be considered as well as mere sport. Indeed the founders have the idea of establishing and training aeronautical volunteers who would be able to give practical training assistance to the authorities for the purpose. An uninterrupted run down to the coast could be obtained and flights of over twenty miles could be attempted.

Another advantage is that on the proposed grounds are several large factory buildings, which could be readily converted into aeroplane erecting sheds and stores while various bungalows in the neighbourhood would give housing for the experimenters.

This report contained two factual errors: the land at Dagenham had been obtained by the Aeronautical Society not the Aero Club, and the area at South Fambridge was 1,600 acres. On the matter of 'the military side of aeronautics', Pemberton Billing had already put a proposal to the War Office for the formation of an 'Imperial Squadron of Aviators', some three years before an Air Battalion was formed!

Never a man to undertake any new project by half measures, Pemberton Billing founded a new monthly journal, *Aerocraft*, mainly to publicise his 'Colony of British Aerocraft'; he was its owner, editor and main writer and also included information about what was going on in the aviation world other than in Britain. The first issue appeared in March just in time for the first Aero and Motor-Boat Exhibition that was held at Olympia in the same month, where he declared that a scale model of his Colony would be on display along with copies of the *Aerocraft*.

Whilst he was at Olympia, Pemberton Billing was approached by a young man, E. Gordon England, who expressed interest in his landing ground. England had already some experience of flying machines through working for another pioneer experimenter – José

José Weiss and his monoplane at South Fambridge. (via R. Davis)

Weiss. Pemberton Billing offered England the post of manager of his Colony at twenty-five shillings a week, which he immediately accepted. Another exhibitor at the show, Richard Lascelles, was also impressed with the project and he and his partner decided to take up one of the workshops at Fambridge. Lascelles was a motor-cycle dealer and planned to set up a spare parts service here; many experimenters used light-weight motor-cycle engines.

Perhaps it was the appointment of Gordon England that persuaded José Weiss to move his monoplane to South Fambridge. Weiss was a Frenchman, who had settled at Amberley in Sussex. He had been a landscape painter and engineer but since 1902 he had been experimenting with flying machines, basing his designs on the shape of a bird's wings. His swept-back wing shape with a curved leading edge had been patented in 1908. His first glider, *Olive*, had been tested on the Sussex Downs by several aviators, including England; because of his advancing years Weiss always used other people to trial his various machines. In 1908 he founded the Weiss

Handley Page (in the top hat) and José Weiss at Olympia in March 1909.

Seton-Karr's biplane at South Fambridge. (via R. Davis)

Aeroplane and Launcher Syndicate and Frederick Handley Page had invested some money in the company; they had first met on the 'Wings Committee' of the Aeronautical Society and at the first Olympia Show they shared a display stand.

After the show Weiss arranged the transport of his small pusher monoplane, *Madge*, to South Fambridge for further tests by his new 'operator' – Gerald Leake. It had a wingspan of 34 ft with distinctive crescent wings and it was powered by a 12 h.p. Anzani engine, which proved to be rather unreliable. The term 'pusher' described a machine where the propeller was sited behind the engine and main wings, whereas if the propeller was located in front of the engine and the wings the machine was described as a 'tractor', i.e. one that pulls the machine along.

Another machine that had also been on display at Olympia was taken to South Fambridge for further trials; it had been built by Howard T. Wright Bros Ltd of Battersea to the order of H. Seton-Karr. It was a rather large and ungainly pusher biplane with a 60 h.p. engine and it was reported to have cost £1,200. Unfortunately whilst in transit by rail it was damaged and later at the landing ground one of its two propellers shattered and they were replaced by a large single propeller. During Seton-Karr's time at South Fambridge he managed to make some straight short hops, which was more than Leake had managed in Weiss's monoplane.

For most of the summer of 1909 these were the only machines at the landing ground except for at least two that Pemberton Billing had designed and built; neither was successful other than in making a few short hops, although he later claimed that he had achieved flight in the second machine. His experiments were not without mishap, one of which landed him in hospital. The summer had been very wet, which made the marshy landing ground even more unsuitable for testing aeroplanes.

Pemberton Billing had decided to rename his Colony – 'The Association of British Aerocraft' – and claimed that several experimenters had applied to come to the landing ground, but only one other aspiring airman did so.

Robert Macfie's monoplane of 1909.

In early August, Robert F. Macfie arrived. He was American-born of Scottish parents and had spent some time in France studying the methods of Wright and Blériot. Within six weeks his tractor monoplane was ready for testing and over the next six weeks or so Macfie had several minor accidents and made a number of modifications to his monoplane, which was powered by a 35 h.p. J.A.P. engine.

Macfie had reluctantly come to the conclusion that South Fambridge was quite unsuitable for taxiing and flying tests. On 11th November he moved his machine to Foulness Island with the objective of using Maplin Sands for his tests. Further damage and bad weather hampered his trials and then the War Office ordered him to leave. He temporarily stored his monoplane in the Kursaal, Southend-on-Sea whilst he arranged shipment to France. Bad luck continued to dog him; his aeroplane was damaged in transit to Paris

A map of the Experimental Flying Ground at Dagenham. (via H.M. Williams)

and the French authorities then refused to allow him to experiment in France. Macfie returned to England and first operated at Portholme near Huntingdon before finding a permanent base at Brooklands. *The Aero* considered his monoplane to be 'comparable with the best of the period'.

Seton-Karr was the first to leave South Fambridge; he moved his biplane to Camber Sands near Rye, where he hoped that he would have better luck. Lascelles also left; the anticipated number of pioneer airmen had not materialised. In October Weiss finally decided to return to his home in Sussex and he was joined there by Gordon England. Pemberton Billing could no longer afford to pay his weekly wage. His Colony or Association had not only proved to be a dismal failure but also a rather costly affair. The last issue of *Aerocraft* appeared in January/February 1910, wherein he informed the readers that he had severed all connections with the journal. Saddled with debts, Pemberton Billing now turned to his second love and for the next three years or so he would largely be engaged in buying, selling and chartering yachts from his new base at Woolston near Southampton before he was once again drawn into the aviation world.

The Aeronautical Society had even less success with their 'Experimental Landing Ground'. During 1908 Colonel Fullerton, the Secretary of the Society, had been urged by some younger members to provide a landing ground where they could work on and trial their flying machines in reasonable seclusion. Largely because they had the active support of the Society's President, Major B.F.S. Baden-Powell, Fullerton was forced to seek a suitable site, although many Society members were opposed to the project. The Colonel found a rough stretch of land alongside the Thames between Barking Creek and Dagenham and to the east of Dagenham Dock that was available for lease from Samuel Williams & Sons Ltd at an annual rent of £50. The Society formed an 'Experimental Ground Committee' comprising eighteen members and chaired by Baden-Powell.

The two-acre site, crossed by drainage ditches and covered in thistles and weeds, was not really suitable for the testing of flying machines. Nevertheless, on 19th January 1909 a lease was signed and later in the month the sub-committee members made a final inspection. It was decided that about an acre would be cleared and levelled and a number of aeroplane sheds, along with a clubhouse, would be erected. Some Society members still retained strong reservations about the suitability of the ground and the expenditure necessary for its preparation. However, they were well aware that the 'upstart' Aero Club was negotiating for a landing ground at Eastchurch. In February tickets and badges were issued and soon the first shed was ready for occupation.

The first to avail himself of the facilities at Dagenham was Major B.F.S. Baden-Powell. The Major, brother of the Chief Scout, had long been involved in aviation matters, mainly concerned with military ballooning and man-lifting kites, although in 1904 he had tested his glider in the grounds of Crystal Palace. Baden-Powell brought his small pusher quadruplane and installed it in one of the sheds; it had a wingspan of 22 ft with a 10/12 h.p. Buchet engine and so far had not flown.

Major Baden-Powell's quadruplane at Dagenham in 1909. (via H.M. Williams)

A.J. Roberts (on the left) and Major B.F.S. Baden-Powell with Moreing's Voisin biplane at Dagenham in 1909. (via H.M. Williams)

He was soon joined by John V. Neale, an electrical engineer from London, who had also been involved with flying machines for at least a decade. He had designed and built a small airship in 1898 but whether it ever became airborne is not recorded. Neale was working on his first aeroplane and took lodgings in nearby Dagenham in order to devote all his time to its construction. Because of its size – a wingspan of a mere 18 ft – Neale had named it *Pup*; it was powered by a 9/12 h.p. J.A.P. engine.

They were joined by G.P. Deverall Saul, who had contracted Handley Page at Woolwich to build his own designed 'tandem' biplane, which was reported to have made several brief and short hops at Dagenham on 25th May when it was piloted by Handley Page himself. Its performance was at least sufficiently encouraging for Saul to order a two-seater version from Handley Page.

The only other member at Dagenham was C.A. Moreing, who brought his large Voisin biplane there. He was a retired mining engineer, who is said to have made a fortune from the Australian gold fields. Moreing was assisted by two Australians, F.J. Healey and A.J. Roberts, both employees of his Australian Electrical Company. Healey was given the task of arranging the construction at Dagenham of a 'large garage' to house Moreing's airship, which had been built by the Spencers. It was 105 ft long with a diameter of 18 ft and whilst it was housed at Dagenham the two Australians were engaged in experiments into the remote radio control of unmanned flying machines. The Voisin was also involved in certain experiments with torpedoes that were conducted at nearby Dagenham Dock.

The single highlight of the landing ground occurred on 18th August when a 'Special Day' was arranged to enable Society members and their guests to inspect the 'first Experimental Landing Ground in the country'. Members of the Press were also invited and 'lots of newspaper reporters and photographers attended'. Most of the eighty or so visitors arrived from London on the Society's 'Aeronautical Special Train', a rather pretentious title for basically a number of open goods wagons from which the elegantly dressed ladies and gentlemen were forced to dismount by way of ladders! Amongst the guests were Lord O'Hagen of Pyrgo Court, Havering-atte-Bower and the Hon. Mrs Assheton-Harbord, a celebrated aeronaut.

Sadly the occasion was not blessed with good weather. Conditions were not suitable for any flying displays but the three aeroplanes were exhibited along with Moreing's airship, although it was not inflated. The following day the *Daily Graphic* carried a long report of 'The Special Day':

Yesterday was set aside by the Aeronautical Society for a visit to the flying ground at Dagenham to discuss future plans. It was not a suitable day for flight so the members inspected the various machines there assembled. To some of the members the new airship dock and Mr Moreing's dirigible balloon were a surprise.

The dirigible is of the non-rigid type and is of Fusiform Shape [spindle-shaped], with the usual protuberances at the tail for stability...Mr Neale's monoplane was visited and the inventor started the engine...

It turned out to be a rather unsatisfactory occasion. One member scathingly dismissed the landing ground as 'a weed preserve' and *The Aero* commented: 'the grounds will need a good deal of improvement before they can be considered good...not a blade of grass was visible.'

By the end of the year the ground had fallen into disuse. Neale moved his monoplane to Brooklands and established one of the first flying training schools there. He was the only pioneer aviator at Dagenham to achieve any modicum of success, building another six machines at his works at Weybridge, Surrey. Moreing sold his Voisin biplane to Eardley Billing (Pemberton Billing's brother) at Brooklands, who used the wings to produce his biplane nicknamed the *Oozley Bird*! However, Moreing's airship remained in storage at Dagenham until the following June. Four years later the airship was placed on display in Sydney, Australia under the control of A.J. Roberts.

The financial loss of the ground at Dagenham created much heated debate within the Society right through 1910. Like Pemberton Billing, the Society had been ill-advised in their choice of site; it would have required a considerable financial outlay to make the land suitable for its purpose. During the 1920s the site was developed by the Ford Motor Company and it became part of their large new car factory.

Elsewhere in Essex, during the summer of 1909 Alliot Verdon Roe was busy trialling his triplane at Lea Marshes near Walthamstow, which was not that far from Dagenham, at least as the crow flies. Roe was born at Patricroft near Manchester in April 1877, the son of a doctor – his mother's maiden name was Verdon, hence his middle name. Rather like Pemberton Billing he was a

Roe's triplane at Lea Marshes in June 1909. A.V. Roe is the second from the right. (Science & Society Picture Library)

much travelled young man, having visited West Africa, Canada and America. During the two years he spent as an engineer at sea, Roe began designing and making model aeroplanes after studying the flight of the albatross. When he finally came ashore Roe briefly worked as Secretary to the Aero Club and in January 1907 he revealed to *The Car* magazine that he was engaged in constructing a full-size flying machine.

Roe submitted no fewer than five models in the *Daily Mail* competition at the Motor Car Exhibition held in the Royal Agricultural Hall in April and was awarded the second prize of £75. This enabled him to finance the construction of his full-size biplane, which he was building in the coachhouse of his brother's house (Dr. Spencer V. Roe) at Putney. By September the biplane had been completed and he was allowed to take it to Brooklands motor racing track to begin tests and trials; Roe's father had been one of the founder members of the Automobile Club, which probably accounts for the permission to use the track. He was attracted by the prize of £1,000 offered by the *Graphic* and *Daily Graphic* for the first flying machine to carry one or more passengers a distance of one mile. These newspapers were owned by George Holt Thomas, then a vigorous business competitor of Lord Northcliffe.

Roe's experiments with his biplane at Brooklands during 1908 are now part of aviation history. He later claimed that on 8th June he succeeded in making several hops at a height of two to three feet, but in 1928/9 a Committee of the Royal Aero Club dismissed his claim to have been the first to fly in Britain on the grounds that he had not been airborne for a sufficient distance; the honour went to Samuel Cody.

Roe returned to Putney with plans to design and build another machine, but this time a triplane. Hitherto his flying experiments

Bull's Eye *triplane at Lea Marshes in July 1909.* (Science & Society Picture Library)

had been largely financed by borrowing money from his family, but on 15th September Roe went into partnership with John A. Prestwich, a well-known motor-cycle manufacturer (J.A.P. Engines). The first engine used on his biplane had been a 6 h.p. J.A.P. but it had proved to be of insufficient power and Roe had arranged for the loan of a French 24 h.p. Antoinette engine. The company, J.A.P. Avroplane, was founded on £100 capital, and fairly soon received its first order – a larger triplane for George Friswell, the agent for Peugeot motor-cars. Prestwich supplied the two engines, a 10 h.p. for Roe's machine and a 35 h.p. for the larger triplane.

During the winter of 1908/9 Roe was fully engaged at Putney building the two triplanes in sections. In the spring of 1909 he needed to find a suitable site to assemble and test them and was convinced that the War Office would allow him to share Farnborough Common where Cody was busy experimenting, but they were 'not disposed to provide facilities for amateur experimenters of aeroplanes...they were a waste of time'!

After an exhaustive search for suitable open land close to London, he finally discovered a couple of derelict railway arches close to Lea Marshes which opened onto an expanse of grassland; the Great Eastern Railway agreed to lease the arches to him at a nominal rent. In March Roe moved into the arches and began to assemble the two triplanes with a number of volunteer helpers, including Tom Narroway, Howard Flanders and E.V.B. Fisher, who later became a fine pilot. Shortly after his move to Lea Marshes, Roe fell out with Friswell about the size of the second triplane and it was never completed by Roe. The incomplete airframe was subsequently auctioned by Friswell and realised just £5.10s.

As there were problems with the new 10 h.p. engine, Roe began, in April, to make the first taxiing trials with his triplane using the original 6 h.p. engine. His triplane was 23 ft long with a wingspan of 20 ft, and its wooden wing spars and ribs were covered with wrapping paper for lightness, to which a coat of yellow varnish had been applied. The side of the triplane carried the name 'Avroplane', the first of a veritable legion of successful Avro aeroplanes; but soon the name *Bulls-Eye* would be added to acknowledge the financial support of his younger brother, Humphrey, who owned a webbing factory in Manchester and whose most successful product was 'Bulls Eye' trouser braces.

Towards the end of May the 10 h.p. engine finally arrived and, from 5th June, Roe managed to get the triplane airborne for brief hops, which he later described as 'dozens of short flights up to 50 feet in length at a height of 2-3 feet, which were hardly more than jumps'. Nevertheless the trials had created considerable local interest and indeed no small amusement; in fact the locals dubbed him 'The Hopper'. Roe's activities had also not gone unnoticed by Leyton Council and they were less than happy with their land being used for 'such dangerous practices', but there was no bye-law to prohibit it.

A.V. Roe flying his triplane in 1909.

On 13th June, after many setbacks, Roe managed to coax his triplane off the ground for a distance of about 100 ft and two days later he achieved another short flight but damaged the undercarriage on landing. On Friday 23rd July he made three flights of about 900 ft at an average height of some 10 ft and thus became the first Briton in the country to fly an all-British aeroplane powered by a British engine. After months upon months of careful and patient tests Roe had achieved his dream.

More flights took place over the next few months which led to mishaps, repairs and several modifications. In October he took his triplane to the Blackpool meeting, along with another similar triplane, but the unfavourable weather meant that neither performed there. When he returned from Blackpool he was given notice to quit the arches and once again he was forced to find another site. He tried the Old Deer Park at Richmond in Surrey, which proved unsuitable, so in November he moved to Wembley Park. His partnership with Prestwich was now amicably dissolved and in January 1910 a private company, A.V. Roe and Company, was formed with the financial support of his brother Humphrey. In March Roe returned to Brooklands, where the new Course Manager, Major Lindsay Lloyd, had converted the centre of the racetrack into an aerodrome, and it had quickly become a veritable colony of pioneer aviators. In 1984 a plaque was unveiled on the railway arches at Lea Marshes, which records Roe's temporary use of them during 1908.

By an odd coincidence another celebrated pioneer aviator, Frederick Handley Page, was also busy at his new works at Creekmouth, close to Barking, during the summer of 1909 – a remarkable period of aviation activity in Essex. Frederick Handley Page was born in Cheltenham on 15th November 1885, the second of four sons; his father ran a furniture and upholstery business but Frederick did not enter the family firm and, against his family's wishes, he moved to London to study electrical engineering at Finsbury Technical College. Throughout his life Frederick used his middle name as if it was part of his surname, which is why 'Handley Page' became such a famous name in British aviation for the next sixty years.

In 1906, at the age of 21, Handley Page was appointed Chief Designer with Johnson & Phillips Ltd, electrical manufacturers based at Charlton in south-east London. Like most young engineers of the time, Frederick was fascinated by the mechanics of flight and in 1907 he joined the Aeronautical Society, which was then rather moribund and in need of reform, having suffered from the formation of the new and progressive Aero Club. Nevertheless the Society provided his entrée into the world of aeronautics and several fellow members were influential when he set up his own business. Very soon he was co-opted onto its 'Wings Committee', where he first met Weiss, who would have a considerable influence on the design of his early aeroplanes. In 1908 Handley Page was dismissed from Johnson & Phillips, apparently for undertaking some of his aeronautical work during office hours.

He immediately established a business at premises in William Street, Woolwich; nothing more grandiose than a small shed and office, but he was prepared to build and test aeroplanes to any required design. Handley Page managed to survive by producing propellers for aeroplanes and airships. His first contract to build an aeroplane came from Deverall Saul and the quadruplane was completed in May 1909. The obvious drawback of his Woolwich works was that there was no open land in the vicinity to trial any gliders and flying machines he might build; therefore he sought a more suitable site for his works and sufficient open land for flying tests and trials.

In early May, Handley Page visited Weiss at South Fambridge, perhaps to get some idea of the landing ground or even, maybe, to consider joining his friend and associate there. Whatever he thought of the facilities and suitability of the landing ground, before the end of the month he had found a site quite close to the Society's ground at Dagenham. It was at Creekmouth near Barking, and had a few acres of land that could be used for trials. He proceeded to erect some buildings, which proudly promoted his new company – Handley Page Ltd; it had been formed on 17th June 1909 for 'the business of manufacturer in aeroplanes, hydroplanes, airships, balloons, aeronautical apparatus and machines'. Not only was it the first company in the country to be formed for the manufacture of aeroplanes, but his works were the first to be specifically built for aeroplane manufacture.

Handley Page already had two orders on hand; a two-seater version of Saul's biplane which the owner hoped to sell for £550 and Major Baden-Powell's latest design, a small 'Scout' monoplane known as *The Midge*, which, when placed on display in November 1910 was noted as belonging to the 'Scout Aero Club'. Handley Page gained some praise and publicity from C.G. Grey in *The Aero* journal for June 1909:

Handley Page's works at Creekmouth near Barking. Saul Quadruplane on its trolley. (via B. Smith)

To illustrate the progress which has been made by our engineers, it is interesting to find that Messrs. Handley Page of Woolwich, have not only gone into the question of aviation thoroughly, but have also gone so far as to appoint agents throughout the Kingdom in connection with flying machines. They recently appointed the Bridgwater Motor Company of Bridgwater, as Agents for the West of England building an aeroplane to enable the Bridgwater Motor Company to give trials flights in their district...

Charles Grey had reported on aviation matters for *The Autocar* since 1906 and was now the joint editor of the new journal, *The Aero*. He became the most dominant and influential voice in aviation journalism until his death in 1953.

The 'aeroplane' was a second biplane similar to the Saul machine but it is not certain whether it was actually built. It is known that Handley Page built his own glider, which was mounted on a tricycle chassis that carried the seated pilot. He made several attempts to get it airborne from Barking but without much success. It is thought that he launched it from one of the dykes that formed a sea wall along the riverside. The glider was later sold to Mr Rodez.

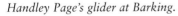
Handley Page's glider at Barking.

Handley Page's Type A, Bluebird, *at Barking in 1909.*

Handley Page's first aeroplane, classified as Type A, was built at Barking during late 1909 and placed on sale at the Olympia Aero Show in March 1910 for £375. It certainly showed the strong influence of Weiss with its pronounced crescent-shaped wings, and it had been named *Bluebird*. Handley Page claimed to have made a few tentative 'hops' with it at Barking on 26th May but in the process the machine was damaged. Whilst it was under repair Handley Page modified the design and replaced the original 20 h.p. engine with a more powerful 50 h.p. Isaacson engine, then reclassified it Type C, although still retaining the original name. Despite the larger engine, Handley Page was unable to get it airborne and ultimately he handed it over (minus the engine) to the Northampton Institute for use as an instructional frame.

W.P. Thompson, a Liverpool patent agent, approached Handley Page to build a biplane that he had designed. During its construction at Barking, Page was assisted by Robert C. Fenwick, Thompson's deputy. He tested the completed biplane at Barking in October but with little success and also it was damaged; further damage was sustained when the shed where it was stored collapsed in a gale. Handley Page viewed it as a failure and referred to it as 'the scrapheap' but he allowed Fenwick to repair and modify it at Barking. In September 1910 Fenwick took it to Freshfields, a landing ground near Liverpool, where by November he had flown it 74 miles and passed his aviator's certificate – No 26; whereupon Handley Page offered him the position of test pilot, which Fenwick gladly accepted.

Of these early experimenters in Essex, only Roe and Handley Page emerged as celebrated aeroplane designers and manufacturers; their companies became household names and were foremost in British aviation over the next sixty or so years.

Chapter 3

Pioneer Experimenters in Essex (1908–1911)

Lea Marshes, South Fambridge, Dagenham and Barking are names that have passed into the annals of pioneer aviation in this country, because of the endeavours of A.V. Roe, Noel Pemberton Billing, Major J.F.S. Baden-Powell and F. Handley Page during 1909. Nevertheless there were several other places in the county that also witnessed scenes of aeronautical activity.

It was a time when, throughout the country, countless numbers of dedicated and determined experimenters were engaged in designing and building flying machines of various shapes and sizes and then bravely trialling them from local fields. Many faced considerable ridicule from the local people, most were labelled 'mad eccentric cranks' by their neighbours and sadly very few were successful in getting airborne. Those that did finally manage to coax their flimsy and dangerous machines off the ground, if only briefly and for however short the distance, no doubt felt that all their hard work and perseverance had been rewarded. The majority have now largely been forgotten except for some cursory reference in the local newspapers of the time and in some instances by a brief acknowledgement of their efforts in subsequent local histories of their towns or villages.

One such man was Jack Edmond Humphreys, who was one of the more intriguing individuals in early Essex aviation and who operated from Wivenhoe between 1908 and 1911. Humphreys was a dentist by profession, hence his nickname – 'the mad dentist' – in aviation circles! He had long been fascinated with the possibilities of flight and had made 'a serious study of birds in flight'; probably from 1902 he had designed and constructed several gliders, one of which is reputed to have carried him a distance of half a mile from cliffs at Coombie Farm at Fowey in Cornwall.

In the autumn of 1908 Humphreys was at Wivenhoe, where an 'amphibious biplane' he had designed was being built at Forrestt & Son's boatyard. He called it an 'aero-hydroplane', a most ambitious venture and probably the first of its kind in the country. The machine was provided with a hull and floats placed at the wing-tips, but for use on land a four-wheel undercarriage was added. In March 1910 it was taken to London by horse and cart to be displayed at the Olympia Aero Show but because of its large wingspan of 45 ft, it could not pass through the doors!

On his return to Wivenhoe Humphreys decided to test it on the Colne, and, on 27th March, a large crowd gathered to see the first trials of the *Wivenhoe Flyer*, as it had been dubbed by the newspapers. The hull was 12 ft 6 ins long and 8 ft broad, the two steel propellers were powered by a 35 h.p. J.A.P. engine and the fuselage was emblazoned with the Union Jack. With Humphreys as pilot, the *Flyer* was launched onto the Colne but it quickly keeled over and remained stranded on the mud. Another attempt was made on 15th April but although it was successfully launched, the gearbox snapped. Three days later it was towed along the river by a local tug, *Dreadnought*, and although it managed to move a short distance under its own power, the *Flyer* failed to take off. A final attempt was made on 14th May but with the same result.

Quite undeterred by these setbacks Humphreys decided to build an aeroplane to compete for the *Daily Mail's* £1,000 prize for the first flight of one mile completed in an all-British machine. To raise the necessary funds to set up a company, he advertised in the national papers during May and June and in the following month the British Aeroplane Syndicate was founded, with its head office in Brook Street, London.

The new monoplane was also built in Wivenhoe and was reported to have cost £300. It was first trialled on unsuitable ground at Wivenhoe on 9th October and managed to move forward some one hundred yards, but struck a drainage ditch and was damaged. The machine was repaired and in November, Humphreys took it to Abbey Fields near Berechurch Road, Colchester, but although he managed to make some fast runs across the ground he was unable to get the machine airborne and, moreover, the propeller was damaged. His efforts were all in vain because, only in the previous month, Moore-Brabazon had claimed and been awarded the coveted *Daily Mail* prize.

Humphreys now refined the design and replaced the original engine with a more robust and powerful 50 h.p. Green engine. The second monoplane, although Humphreys referred to it as 'an improved earlier version', was taken to Bournemouth in July 1910 to fly in what was advertised as the 'First International Air Meeting in the country', but it actually did not fly there, nor indeed at the Blackpool meeting later in the year. Humphreys now decided to join the growing band of aspiring aviators attracted to Brooklands, where he rented Hangar No 10, and soon his machine was dubbed

Jack Humphreys' No 2 monoplane at Wivenhoe.

The Elephant by fellow experimenters, presumably for its size; with a wingspan of 48 ft it was one of the largest aeroplanes at Brooklands.

His third monoplane was also built at Wivenhoe although it was taken to Brooklands for trials, where it was described as 'a Blériot type'. On 4th February 1911, the Hon. Mrs Assheton-Harbord formally named it *Mary* in honour of the new Queen. During May and June, Humphreys was known to be taking flying lessons at the Hanriot Flying School, just one of a number of schools then active at Brooklands, but he never gained his aviator's certificate. Nevertheless, on 30th August he managed to get his monoplane airborne but only to a height of about ten feet before it crashed and was severely damaged.

After quite major repairs C. Gordon Bell, a well-known pilot who had also been instructed by the Hanriot School, succeeded in getting it airborne with, according to reports, 'two or three passengers' (possibly including Jack Humphreys). In early January 1912, one of his mechanics was seriously injured whilst swinging the propeller. Later in the month another young Brooklands' pilot, James Hunter, made several flights in the monoplane, which was now powered by a 60 h.p. Green engine.

On 12th May, Humphreys was at the controls and was taxiing along to the sheds at Brooklands when he collided with an aeroplane belonging to the Hewlett & Blondeau School of Flying and both aeroplanes were completely destroyed. It was said at the time that Humphreys had been greatly upset by some adverse criticism concerning his ability (or rather lack of it!) as a pilot, which appeared in *The Aeroplane*. Perhaps because of this rather harsh censure, and the considerable amount of money he had already spent on his various machines, Humphreys decided to withdraw from the aviation scene and return to dentistry; he established a practice in Harley Street, London.

For two years Clacton-on-Sea (or more precisely, Little Clacton) was the scene of flying experiments in machines constructed in the town. In 1909, Guy Laking, the son of Sir Francis Laking, physician to King Edward VII, had become fascinated with flying and he specified and financed the construction of a biplane. Laking sought out the help of T.W.K. Clarke of Kingston-upon-Thames with the design of his flying machine. Clarke had been involved in building model aeroplanes and gliders since 1906 and now he was prepared to build any aeroplane to a customer's design for the sum of £200 but without an engine, which would be provided by the customer.

Although Laking's biplane, known as *Laking 1*, was built by Clarke, the assembly was entrusted to A. Fitch & Son, Motor Engineers of Rosemary Street, Clacton-on-Sea, and more particularly supervised by Frank Fitch. The first notice of the biplane occurred in October 1909 when details of the machine appeared in the aeronautical press. It had a wingspan of 33 ft and was powered by *two* 12 h.p. J.A.P. engines. This was a unique design; hitherto no other pioneer aeroplane had been designed to be twin-engined.

By the end of the year the assembly of *Laking 1* was completed, but Guy Laking had lost interest in the project and was travelling in Europe, apparently leaving his interest in his biplane to Frank Fitch, who now proceeded to reconstruct it. He converted it to a single

Laking biplane No 1 at Little Clacton in July 1911. (via L.T. Smith)

engine – a 40 h.p. Lascelles. In June 1911 Fitch rented a field at Bocking Elm, Little Clacton where a small shed was erected for the final assembly of *Laking 1*, as it was still called; in fact, 'The Laking Biplane No 1' was boldly emblazoned on the tail.

On 4th July *Laking 1* made its first flight in the hands of Anthony Westlake, who was also an automobile engineer and engine designer. He achieved a circular flight of some three hundred yards at a height of about fifteen feet and a speed of about twenty m.p.h. and successfully landed back on the field from where he had taken off, which was no mean feat in those early flying days. In all the excitement of this successful first flight, it was reported that a second flight would take place in Colchester and, furthermore, that a passenger would be carried. There were also plans to establish a flying school at Little Clacton, but for whatever reasons none of these projects materialised.

Westlake had apparently been interested in aeronautics since 1904, largely designing and building gliders, although one report suggests that in March 1911 he had built a biplane based on the lines of a Cody machine, powered by his own 18 h.p. engine; it is

Piggott Brothers' first biplane was built at Stanford Rivers in 1910. (via L.T. Smith)

unfortunate that there seems to be no existing record to show where this machine was built or indeed whether it ever flew. It was left to Westlake to continue flying at Little Clacton.

The small and sleepy village of Stanford Rivers, to the south of Chipping Ongar, might be considered one of the more unlikely places in the county to be the site of manufacture of several aeroplanes during 1910 to 1912, but it was at this village that Piggott Bros & Co Ltd of Bishopsgate Street, London decided to enter into the world of aviation. Their 'No 1 Biplane' was built in early 1910; it had been designed by S.C. Parr. The large biplane (wingspan of 60 ft and over 34 ft in length) was a side-by-side two-seater and was provided with a powerful 80 h.p. Vinius engine. It was later taken to Hendon for testing but there is no evidence that it ever left the ground.

The company now built a monoplane, again to Parr's design, which was exhibited at the Olympia Aero Show in April 1911. It was one of the first aeroplanes to provide an enclosed cockpit for the pilot, although it was later modified to an open cockpit; in fact the engine was also enclosed as well as the accommodation for passengers, quite a sophisticated design. It was powered by the same

Piggott Brothers' monoplane on display at Olympia in 1911. (via L.T. Smith)

Vinius engine, which was claimed to give it a top speed of 75 m.p.h.; Parr again tested this monoplane at Hendon but the undercarriage was severely damaged during the trials and it was apparently abandoned. The manufacture of aeroplanes was merely a side-line; the company's main business was producing canvas tents and marquees although it had quickly branched out into aeroplane sheds. The company's final attempt to produce a monoplane that did actually fly came in 1912 and is detailed in the following chapter.

There were a number of other intrepid individuals working on their own machines up and down the county, but the surviving records and references to their vain efforts are very sparse and scattered. Victor F.E. Forbes and Arthur J. Arnold, both of Leigh-on-Sea, registered a patent (No 20846) in 1909 for a design of a monoplane but it was not completed until late 1910 when details

Victor Forbes and Arthur Arnold's monoplane at Leigh-on-Sea in 1910.

appeared in *Flight* journal. It was a rather flimsy construction built of bamboo and was thought to have been powered by a motor-car engine, which being water-cooled required a radiator; *Flight* commented '[it] proved to be too heavy for the machine'. The monoplane was reported to have made a brief flight at Rochford, though it was not stated whether Forbes or Arnold was at the controls, nor indeed the precise place where this took place. Nothing further is noted about the monoplane or the two men.

Considering all the flying activity taking place at Handley Page's factory at Barking, it is not surprising to find that another two experimenters from Barking, E.S.B. Mackensie-Hughes and A.W. Smith, were busy building their rather complicated triplane, which Mackensie-Hughes had designed. Perhaps they hoped to emulate Handley Page? Their triplane was taken to Brooklands in June 1910, where it was housed in Hangar 22, with *Britannia* emblazoned in large letters along its fuselage. It was probably built with the *Daily Mail* £1,000 prize in mind. During its trials at Brooklands in July and August, fellow aviators dubbed it 'the

Staircase' because its wings were staggered like steps. Unfortunately it never left the ground; according to a report it was 'far too heavy and grossly underpowered'; it had a 20 h.p. J.A.P. engine. However, Smith and Mackensie-Hughes managed to sell the aeroplane to a H.B. Holesworth, who proceeded to convert it to a biplane with a 60 h.p. E.N.V. engine, but all his attempts to get it airborne at Brooklands during the spring of 1911 also failed.

Early in 1911 Handley Page was concentrating on the design of his fourth aeroplane – Type D – another crescent-winged monoplane. He had also been searching around Barking for a different landing ground that he could use for his flying trials and finally managed to rent part of large playing fields at Fairlop Oak alongside Forest Road, where he erected a shed for the storage and preparation of his aeroplanes. Certainly the large area of level and smooth grass was much more favourable for his fragile machines than the rough and uneven surface at Barking. Henceforth all the flying tests of his aeroplanes would be conducted from Fairlop.

Type D was displayed at the Olympia Aero Show in April 1911 and offered for sale at £450, the price including free flying tuition. It was slightly longer than its predecessor with a greater wingspan and was equipped with a 35 h.p. Green engine, which Handley Page had borrowed. The monoplane was not sold, probably due to the fact that Robert Fenwick had been unable to get it airborne. After the show the Green engine was replaced with a 60 h.p. Isaacson engine and Handley Page entered it into the *Daily Mail* Circuit of Britain race due to start on 22nd July. Fenwick finally managed to complete some flights from Fairlop on 15th July but he crashed on landing, heavily damaging the aeroplane, which meant that the machine would not be ready for the race; Handley Page immediately sacked Fenwick!

His new test pilot was Edward Petre; he and his elder brother by two years, Henry Aloysius, had some previous experience of aeroplane design and flying at Brooklands. They had built a monoplane in Hangar No 11, which Henry had managed to get

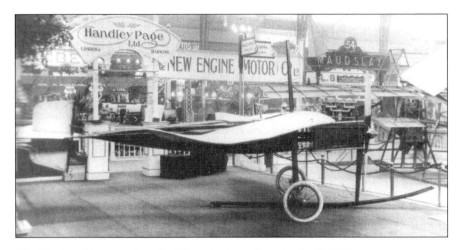

The Handley Page stand at the Olympia Aero Show in April 1911.

Captain Edward M. Maitland of the Essex Regiment commanded No 1 Company of the Air Battalion.

Edward Petre – 'Peter the Painter' – qualified for his Royal Aero Club Certificate (No 259) at Fairlop. (R.A.F. Museum)

airborne to a height of 23 feet and for a distance of some one hundred yards. However, a strong gust of wind caused the monoplane to crash and the brothers decided not to rebuild it.

Nevertheless, Henry obtained his aviator's certificate, No 128, on 12th September 1911 whilst flying a Hanriot monoplane at Brooklands, whereas, as yet, Edward was uncertificated. They were, of course, scions of the famous Essex Petre family of Thorndon and Ingatestone Halls and two of the five sons of Sebastian H. Petre of Tor Bryan, Ingatestone. It is believed that they had invested some money in Handley Page Ltd in order that they might have some say in future designs. Edward was said to be 'a most charming and likeable man, who had a way of his own' and in aviation circles he became known as 'Peter the Painter' from the infamous criminal of the recent Sydney Street siege; Henry had also acquired a nickname – 'The Monk' – but it is not known for what reason.

During the rebuild of the aeroplane, the fabric surfaces were varnished yellow; Edward Petre dubbed the aeroplane *Antiseptic* but it became more popularly known as *Yellow Peril* from the well-known Gold Flake cigarettes, because of their yellow packets. Petre managed to make a few short flights in it from Fairlop.

However, the facility of a wind tunnel at the Northampton Institute in London was used to refine the aerodynamics of Handley

Gratze's monoplane, Daisy, *in 1910.*

Page's next machine. For some months Handley Page had lectured on aeronautical engineering to the Institute's students on two evenings a week. He had certainly made a mark on the aviation world; in September he had been made an Associate Fellow of the Aeronautical Society and had been elected to its Council. Nevertheless he was now fully engaged on his Type E, a two-seat monoplane which was about 6 ft longer and had an increased wingspan. Although it would not be ready for testing until 1912 he had decided to purchase a rather expensive 50 h.p. Gnôme engine; a French aero-engine, considered one of the best available.

There was at least one *known* Essex man active in designing gliders and powered machines before 1909 – W.J. Potter of Elysia, Woodham Ferrers. His monoplane design was built during 1909 by the Ariel Manufacturing Company of Finsbury, London. Towards the end of the year Alec Ogilvie, a celebrated pioneer aviator, managed to achieve several flights at Camber Sands near Rye in Sussex, the longest being about two hundred and fifty yards. Perhaps buoyed with this success, in January 1910 the Ariel Company advertised aeroplanes for sale with such patriotic names as *The British King, The British Queen* and *The Flying Scotsman* but whether they were designed by Potter is not recorded, or even if they were built. Potter is known to have registered patents for another monoplane and three biplanes during 1910. There is no evidence that the company sold a single aeroplane and it apparently slipped out of the aviation world. On the other hand Potter, who was obviously well-known in aviation circles, was sought out by Ernest Willows of Cardiff, who was then one of the leading airship builders. He contracted Potter to complete the envelope for his third and latest airship, *City of Cardiff,* which first flew on 26th October 1910.

Another Essex village, Canewdon, was selected as the site for the trials of what was described as 'a dirigoplane'. Eugene V. Gratze Ltd of Whitfield Street, London had designed and built a monoplane in time to appear at the Blackpool air meeting in October 1909. However, whilst being carried by rail to Blackpool the wings were lost in transit. Gratze proceeded to modify his machine, which he named *Daisy* and in November he managed to get it airborne with a 40 h.p. J.A.P. engine. During May 1910 he moved *Daisy* to Canewdon to undertake further trials, which appear to have been successful, because at the end of 1911 *Daisy* was advertised for sale as 'a proven flyer'. The asking price was £80 though Gratze is reported as saying that it had cost him £800 to build – quite a fortune in those days. He is yet another one of those early experimenters that suddenly disappeared from the aviation world.

The names of a few other Essex flying enthusiasts appear fleetingly in the several aeronautical journals of the time. A Chingford man, 'J.C. Locke of Buxton Road', had completed 'a tail-less glider with large swept-back wings', which he had successfully tested at Barking in July 1910. Perhaps this was the same spot on Barking marshes where Handley Page had tested his first glider.

Even the county town, Chelmsford, managed to get into the aviation scene, albeit very briefly. Moore-Brabazon, who had been active with A.V. Roe at Brooklands during 1908 with his powered biplane glider, brought it to Chelmsford after he had been asked to leave Brooklands. He had removed the Buchet engine and a report stated that 'he briefly used it as a kite being towed by a motor-car'. It is not known where in Chelmsford he trialled his glider. Soon he left for Paris where he received flying instruction and also purchased a Voisin aeroplane, which he called *The Bird of Passage*. Some three years later there is a reference to 'Ross of Hilgay Park Road, Chelmsford' who offered his Blériot-type monoplane for sale in the 28th January 1911 edition of *Flight*. Again one can only wonder where Mr Ross stored his monoplane.

Two months later the same journal reported that 'Mr Buckle of Lexden, Colchester' was the designer of a monoplane with a 30 ft wingspan, which 'will be trialled in the near future'. However, there is no further record that this machine ever flew. Despite the fact that the majority of these attempts at powered flight were unsuccessful, they nevertheless clearly demonstrated that the spirit of aviation was alive in the county, and furthermore many people in Essex had witnessed these strange and rather fragile machines or 'aerial cars'.

The year 1911 was a landmark one for British military aviation. On 28th February an Army order was issued which created an Air Battalion of the Royal Engineers with effect from 1st April. The Air Battalion comprised two Companies; No 1 (Airships, balloons and kites) to be based at Farnborough and No 2 (Aeroplanes) at Larkhill.

There was an Essex link with the establishment of the country's first military air force; Captain Edward Maitland, who was given the command of No 1 Company, was then serving in the Essex Regiment. He had joined the Regiment in May 1900 as Second Lieutenant E.M. Gee and served in the South African War with the 2nd Battalion. In July 1903 he changed his surname to Maitland, perhaps as a condition of a family inheritance? Maitland (or Gee!) had long been an enthusiast of ballooning and airships and was a member of the Aeronautical Society. During 1909 he was reported to be 'trying for the £4,000 prize to fly across the Channel in an all-British machine', and by 1910 he was at Brooklands with his Howard Wright biplane, but on 1st August he crashed and sustained several injuries including a broken leg.

However, Maitland is best remembered for his pioneering work with parachutes and his long and dedicated support for their use in the Royal Flying Corps and later the Royal Air Force. He made his first parachute descent from a balloon in 1908 and in July 1913 Maitland was the first person to make a parachute jump from an airship – *Beta 11*. He rose steadily through the ranks of the R.F.C./R.A.F. and by 1921 he was an Air Commodore and decorated with the C.M.G., D.S.O. and D.F.C.; in July 1919 he was one of the 22 airmen that made a successful double crossing of the Atlantic in the airship, R.34.

Sadly he was one of the 44 persons on board the R.38 when it broke up and exploded in flames over the river Humber on 23rd August 1921; ironically all on board were equipped with parachutes

Howard Flanders' F3 with an early Marconi wireless.

Handley Page's Type E was flown from Fairlop in 1911.

but because of the speed of the disaster there was no time to use them and only five survived. Maitland was aged 41 years at his death and he is commemorated on a pew end at the Essex Regiment's Chapel at Warley near Brentwood. All his pioneering and dedicated work on parachutes finally came to fruition when, in 1927, seat-pack parachutes were brought into general use in the Royal Air Force.

The year had opened with the formation of the Military Wing and now closed with the War Office's announcement (in December) that there was to be a competition for 'machines suitable for military operations' with formal ground flying trials to be held in the summer of 1912. It was not really the prize money that was on offer – £4,000 for the overall winner and £1,000 for the best British machine – that attracted the competitors, but rather the strong probability of a lucrative military contract. The military trials concentrated the minds of aeroplane companies and individuals alike for the next six months or so, including Piggott Bros & Co Ltd and Handley Page Ltd.

Chapter 4

Aviation Events in Essex (1912 to August 1914)

I n 1912 Howard Flanders, one of A.V. Roe's early assistants and now an aeroplane manufacturer, affirmed: 'Aviation is now passing into a new phase.' The days of the 'amateur' experimenters had all but drawn to a close, such had been the rapid and significant progress in all aspects of aviation since 1910.

Those dedicated individuals who had beavered away with their machines in wooden sheds and back gardens had virtually disappeared into obscurity. Some had moved to continue their experiments and trials either to Brooklands or Hendon, which were considered *the* centres of aviation in the country. Aeroplane manufacture had markedly increased and the number of companies that had been founded to capitalise on this novel world of air transport were sufficiently numerous to be described as an industry, albeit in a rather embryonic form. Nevertheless several companies that would figure large in British aviation in the years ahead can trace their origins back to these years – Armstrong Whitworth, Blackburn, Bristol and Vickers had now joined the pioneering companies of Avro, Handley Page and the Short Brothers.

After September 1912 when Handley Page moved his factory from Barking to Cricklewood, north London, there were only two *known* aeroplanes designed and built in Essex. The public interest that had been created in the county by Roe, Handley Page, Humphreys, Westlake *et al* would have to be satisfied with the occasional appearances of such flying 'stars' as Claude Grahame-White, Benny Hucks, Gustav Hamel and 'Boy' Manton. The formation of the Royal Flying Corps (R.F.C.) in April at least offered the opportunity to young flying enthusiasts to enlist and enter this thrilling world; nevertheless, by the end of 1912, there were only 282 certificated pilots in the whole of the country, so flying remained a small and exclusive world.

The R.F.C. had been proposed by the Committee of Imperial Defence, which in late 1911 had been given the task of considering 'the future development of aerial navigation for naval and military purposes…and to propose measures that would create an efficient and effective aerial force'. The proposed Corps would include Military and Naval Wings, along with a Central Flying School. On 13th April 1912 a Royal Warrant was issued for the constitution of the R.F.C. and one month later it came into being. King George V agreed to the Royal appellation 'in consideration of the especially difficult and arduous nature of the flying service'.

Most of the entrants into the R.F.C. were already serving Army personnel and several officers and men of the Essex Regiment took the opportunity to transfer to the new force. It would be another twelve months or so before direct recruitment for men between the ages of 18 and 30 years commenced; they could join as air mechanics at a basic rate of 2s (10p) per day, but if they were trained as 'flyers' they received an additional 2s per day.

A recruitment poster for the Military Wing, Royal Flying Corps.

For the first time any young man, from however lowly circumstances, could enter this new discipline, which hitherto had been mainly the preserve of relatively few, those fortunate enough to be able to afford the expense of flying tuition and the high costs of buying and maintaining an aeroplane. John Barfoot in *Essex Airmen 1910–1918* lists some 250 Essex-born men who served in the R.F.C./R.A.F. during World War One. Perhaps the most celebrated was Donald W. Clappen of Westcliff-on-Sea, who obtained his R.Ae.C (591) in August 1913 and finally retired from the RAF in 1949 at the rank of Air Commodore.

Perhaps the most significant aviation event in Essex during 1912 also occurred during April at Handley Page's small flying field at Fairlop. On the 26th, Edward Petre made the first hops in Handley Page's Type E and he soon progressed to complete circuits. Once Petre was satisfied with the aeroplane's flying qualities, he flew it from Fairlop to Barking, some six miles, but the machine sustained some damage landing on the rough ground at Barking. At this time Petre had not yet qualified for his aviator's certificate but this was rectified on 24th July when he successfully passed all the flying tests at Fairlop: the first time any pilot had obtained his certificate (No 259) whilst flying from a landing ground in Essex.

Three days later Petre flew the Type E, which had inherited the name *Yellow Peril*, because of its yellow wings and tail, from Fairlop to Brooklands in just 50 minutes. It was the first ever flight across London and ensured the aeroplane's success. Handley Page claimed that it was 'so easy to fly and so comfortable is the disposition of the seating and controls, that for real pleasure in flying this machine is unsurpassed'. Over the next two years the aeroplane flew over two thousand miles and carried several hundred passengers. Handley Page had also purchased the assets of the Aeronautical Syndicate Ltd from its founder, Horatio Barber, who had built no less than twenty machines since 1909, but had not sold a single one. Handley Page Ltd was certainly now well established in the vanguard of British aviation.

Wedding guests on the lawn of Hylands House with two aeroplanes in the background.

Another aviation event in Essex caused considerable public interest. On 26th June 1912 St Mary's church at Widford, a small village on the outskirts of Chelmsford, was the scene of a most remarkable 'society' wedding that made front page news not only nationally but internationally, such was the universal fame and popularity of the bridegroom, Claude Grahame-White. He was the most celebrated aviator in the land and the British press heralded it as the 'first air-wedding'. The sumptuous wedding reception was held at nearby Hylands House, then owned by Sir Daniel and Lady Mary Gooch.

Grahame-White came from a wealthy Hampshire family and had trained as an engineer. Like most well-to-do young men, he was fascinated with motor-cars and became an early member of the Automobile Club. By 1905 he had established a flourishing car dealership at Albermarle Street, London. However, as he later admitted, what changed his life for ever was Blériot's successful crossing of the English Channel and more so his visit to the Reims air meeting in August 1909. Enthralled and excited by the flying he

Claude Grahame-White – the 'Matinee Idol of the Air'.

A special postcard was issued to commemorate the wedding of Claude Grahame-White and Dorothy Taylor.

witnessed there, he immediately ordered a Blériot XII and he even persuaded Blériot, normally very secretive concerning his construction methods, to spend eight weeks at his factory whilst his aeroplane was being built. On 6th November he astonished onlookers by flying solo in his Blériot, *White Eagle,* without any previous instruction; he was obviously a 'born aviator'. Early in January 1910 he was awarded his French *brevet de pilote-aviateur* (No 30) – the first Briton to hold an internationally recognised aviator's certificate. Grahame-White also opened a flying school at Pau in southern France, the first-ever British flying training school albeit on foreign soil.

Returning to Britain, Grahame-White joined all the other famous aviators at Brooklands, where he rented Hangar 16. He was relatively unknown in this country but that would soon alter most dramatically. In April 1910 he famously raced against the French aviator, Louis Paulham, for the *Daily Mail's* £10,000 prize for the first flight from London to Manchester, during which Grahame-White became the first airman to fly by night. The race captured the public's imagination and the progress of the two airmen gripped the country's attention; it was billed as 'The Race of the Century'.

Although Paulham won, Grahame-White had gained overnight popularity; he was in great demand to give exhibition flights and had become the country's first 'aviation hero'. He was tall, handsome and debonair with an abundance of natural charm, which made him a great favourite with society ladies, who vied to be a passenger in his new Farman biplane. Grahame-White was so utterly convinced about the glorious future for aeroplanes and more especially for military purposes that in July he rather audaciously flew over the Grand Fleet gathered in Mount's Bay off Cornwall and dropped an 'imaginary bomb' on the flagship HMS *Dreadnought* as a practical demonstration of the aeroplane's potential as a new weapon of war.

After competing in the various air meetings during that summer, in September Grahame-White sailed from Liverpool on the White Star liner, *Cymric,* bound for the Boston-Harvard air meeting, the first American 'air meet' of any consequence; A.V. Roe was also on board. Grahame-White was not only very successful at Boston but also in New York and by the time he returned to England he had amassed over $250,000 in prize money, exhibition and passenger fees. He had equally charmed the American ladies; it was reported that they were prepared to pay $500 for a passenger flight with 'the matinee idol of the air', as the American press had dubbed him! From now on Grahame-White's name was hardly ever out of the newspapers and the Aerial League awarded him a Gold Medal for his 'services for aviation'. Grahame-White returned to the United States the following year, though not with the same marked success.

Without doubt his lasting claim to fame was the development of a small landing ground at Hendon, north London, into what he called 'London Aerodrome', which was formally opened in March

1911. Largely due to his flair as a publicist, Hendon soon became a Mecca of aviation for the huge crowds that came to watch the various air displays and races that he staged there. Grahame-White also attracted well-known London socialites, so much so that Hendon fast became a social venue to rival Ascot and Henley. His flying school instructed many aviators, both young and old, and male and female; he also went into the business of aircraft construction and formed the Grahame-White Aviation Co Ltd.

In early May 1912 Grahame-White gave a spectacular display of flying over the Fleet that had gathered in Portland Bay for the Royal Review. It was another well-publicised event, where as the *Daily Mail* reported, 'the two airmen flew round and round the warships so near the water as to be scarcely visible above the level of the decks and demonstrated supreme skill in controlling and flying their aeroplanes'. Only weeks before his marriage Grahame-White staged the first Aerial Derby, held at Hendon on 8th June, and over 45,000 people attended the start of the race. Thus it is not surprising that his wedding created such intense public interest.

His bride was Miss Dorothy Taylor, a New York heiress, and amongst the guests were most of the leading airmen of the day. Several had arrived in their aeroplanes and landed on the lawns of the large country house. Quite naturally Grahame-White arrived by air, in one of Cody's large biplanes, *Cathedral*, which Cody had loaned him for the day. As the couple emerged from Widford church, Benny Hucks flew overhead and dropped confetti. After the lavish reception at Hylands House the other guests (close to two hundred) were treated to an impromptu flying display by such stars as Hucks, Hamel, Robert Loraine, Pierre Verrier and Thomas Sopwith. It was a notable first, a quite remarkable occasion considering it was less than three years since the first powered flights in Britain. Many of the newspaper reports boldly claimed that 'the aeroplane has truly come of age'!

After a brief honeymoon Grahame-White returned to flying and during July and August 1912 he, along with other aviators, set off

"DAILY MAIL" WATERPLANE TOUR, 1912.
ORGANISED BY THE GRAHAME WHITE AVIATION CO., LTD.
70 H.P. HENRY FARMAN WATERPLANE.

on an extensive 'Wake Up, England' (his motto) tour, which his company promoted jointly with the *Daily Mail*. The object of the displays, according to Lord Northcliffe, 'was to educate the people of this country as to the qualities and potentialities of the new arm and to stimulate the Government and the War Office to make up for the deficiency of past neglect'. Special emphasis was placed on the waterplane and for this reason Grahame-White had purchased a Farman 'hydro-aeroplane', which could be flown with either a wheeled undercarriage or floats. It was painted in a vivid blue with 'Wake Up, England' boldly emblazoned on its wings and fuselage.

Grahame-White started his tour of seaside resorts along the south coast, when the *Tatler* magazine complained that the resorts were 'overrun with hydroplanes...evangels of the *Daily Mail* preaching the gospel of flight...Mr Grahame-White's name is on everyone's lips. He is the hero of the hour.' The 'hero' arrived at Southend-on-Sea on 26th August, where he was joined by his wife. It was reported that the seafront was crammed with people eager to see his

Handley Page's monoplane 'No 28' for the Military Trials of August 1912.

display. Two days later the couple left for Clacton-on-Sea and they landed on the sea at the Marine Parade and then calmly adjourned to the Grand Hotel where they lunched with Lady Gooch, who was spending a few days by the sea. In the afternoon thousands gathered along the Marine Parade to watch a really splendid exhibition of flying before Grahame-White continued northwards on his tour. In total he and his other pilots visited over 120 towns, gave 500 exhibition flights and carried some 1,200 passengers.

A second 'Wake Up England' tour during the following summer was not so extensive and attracted less attention. The lack of interest, according to Grahame-White, was not too disappointing: maybe it showed that 'the British public had finally accepted the aeroplane so much so that they had become a little *blasé* about them'. Sad to relate, the Grahame-Whites' marriage lasted just four years: they divorced in December 1916. However, Hylands House has survived; the house and its surrounding parkland is now owned and in the process of restoration by Chelmsford Borough Council. The park is open to the public during daylight hours and at the time of writing the house is open to visitors on Sundays and Mondays.

Away from these very public air displays, the companies and individuals involved in aeroplane construction were intent on the imminent Military Trials at Larkhill on Salisbury Plain. Handley

Page had modelled his entry on the Type E, although still powered by a Gnôme engine, and it was designated Type F. Piggott Brothers produced a two-seater biplane, again designed by Parr, which was equipped with a 35 h.p. Anzani engine. After a delay of about a month to allow certain manufacturers to prepare their aeroplanes, the long-awaited Trials finally commenced on 4th August. There were thirty-two entrants, both British and foreign, of which eighteen were British-built but only four were also powered with British engines. It is perhaps a little surprising to find that two of these aeroplanes had been built in Essex and coincidentally they were numbered '28' and '29'. As just three British companies, A.V. Roe, Bristol and Coventry Ordnance, had entered a total of eight machines, it might be said that the county was well represented.

The Piggott biplane, flown by Parr, did not qualify for the flying tests but Handley Page's Type F did. Henry Petre was originally entered as its pilot but he had expressed some concern about the remodelled wings; they were less swept-back and placed higher on the fuselage than previous models, which Handley Page felt had made it far more stable. Petre had also been successful in being selected for the proposed Australian Flying School and Flying Corps and perhaps his contract forbade him flying for Handley Page. His brother, Edward, was more than happy to replace him as the pilot.

The monoplane had arrived late when most of the competitors had completed the flying tests. However, on 21st August Petre completed a preliminary flying test and the following day it entered the Trials. Sadly the engine, a 70 h.p. Gnôme which was fully enclosed for the first time, failed, and as Petre attempted to make a landing downwind in gusty conditions he was forced to avoid a group of people. The wing hit the ground and was smashed; the plane took no further part in the competition. Perhaps to the surprise of most aviation experts the overall winner was Samuel Cody's large Biplane 5. The Trials were marred by the tragic death of Robert Fenwick, Handley Page's ex-test pilot, whilst flying a Mersey monoplane.

The damaged Type F was not returned to Barking for repairs, it was stored at Brooklands pending the company's imminent move. For several months Handley Page had been actively seeking new premises. The factory space at Barking was rather restricted, especially as orders for propellers and other aeroplane material had steadily increased, irrespective of the prospect of aeroplane orders in the wake of the successful Type E, and also the landing ground at Barking had long been found unsuitable for test flying. Besides, the company had recently been awarded a sub-contract to build a number of Royal Aircraft Factory's BE.2a scout aircraft, which had been designed by Geoffrey de Havilland; although in fact for various reasons the company only built three.

In September 1913 Handley Page Ltd moved to former riding stables at Cricklewood, north London which were within easy reach of Hendon aerodrome. Thus after three eventful years Handley Page left Barking. His company ultimately produced some of the country's most famous aircraft, civil and military, until it went into receivership in February 1970. Like A.V. Roe, Frederick Handley Page became one of the leading figures of British aviation; he was knighted in 1942 and died in April 1962 aged 76.

As the year came to a close there were two fatal accidents that particularly affected Handley Page. The Type F crashed on 15th December whilst on a flight from Hendon to Oxford; Lieutenant William Parke, R.N. and his passenger A. Arkell Hardwick, Handley Page's works manager, were both killed. Nine days later (24th) Edward Petre was flying a Martin Handasyde 65 h.p. monoplane from Brooklands to Edinburgh; since leaving Handley Page he had been employed by the Martin Handasyde Company at Brooklands as a test pilot. The weather on the journey north became increasingly stormy and it was thought that Petre was attempting an emergency landing at Marske-by-the-Sea in Yorkshire but he crashed and was killed. The Royal Aero Club's investigation into the tragic accident found that the wings had collapsed in flight.

Whatever aviation progress had been made during the year, it had been achieved at some cost in human lives. Several military airmen had been killed in accidents, along with a number of celebrated pioneer aviators, an indication that there were still many improvements to be made in the safety of aeroplanes and especially the reliability of aero-engines.

In 1913 Anthony Westlake formed the East Anglian Aviation Company, with its head office situated in Shaftesbury Avenue, London, but its works housed in a building in Clacton-on-Sea, said to be 'next to the waterfront', although Westlake's home address was then shown as Great Ormond Street, Bloomsbury, London. His new machine was described as 'an elegant monoplane'; it was a single-seat tractor with a wingspan of 34 ft, over 23 ft long and its main feature was a large fan-shaped tail plane. It was powered by an 18 h.p. engine which he had designed.

During the summer the monoplane was trialled by Westlake at Bockings Elm, Little Clacton. By September he had managed to make several short straight flights but none of any appreciable distance. According to a report in the aeronautical press, his monoplane showed 'some promise, but it is sadly underpowered'.

Anthony Westlake's monoplane in 1913. (via K. Evans)

Deperdussin Seagull *on test – River Blackwater, July 1913.* (via K. Evans)

Nevertheless on 20th October it was offered for sale by auction along with 'a spare Lascelles aero-engine' (maybe the *Laking 1* engine?). The name of the purchaser was not recorded, if in fact it was sold. I have not found any record that Westlake built another machine.

During the summer there were other flying trials taking place in Essex. In July, Osea Island in the Blackwater was used to test a new waterplane, *Seagull*, which had been manufactured by the British Deperdussin Aeroplane Company Ltd of Stoke Newington. The company had been formed in April 1912 to design and build monoplanes similar to those of its parent French company. One of the British directors and also test pilot was Lieutenant J.C. Porte, R.N., a well-known pioneer aviator. At the outbreak of the war Porte was made the Commander of the Royal Naval Air Service's station at Hendon, but because of his pre-war connection with the American designer Glenn Curtiss, he would be instrumental in introducing flying boats into military use, especially against German U-boats.

Seagull was the first original design of the British company and was the product of its Chief Designer, Frederick Koolhaven, a Dutchman. It had been exhibited at the Aero Show at Olympia in

February 1913 priced at £1,500, and the Admiralty were sufficiently impressed with the prototype to place an order for two. Indeed, by March nine Deperdussin monoplanes had been ordered by the War Office from the British company at a total cost of £8,473, but none of them was particularly successful operationally.

The waterplane or floatplane was basically a landplane which had been fitted with a broad central float. *Seagull* had a wingspan of over 42 ft and was 30 ft long; it was powered by a 100 h.p. Anzani engine, which was claimed to give it a top speed of 55 m.p.h. In those days the Admiralty (and indeed Lord Northcliffe) were convinced that in the event of war, waterplanes flying from bases along the east and south-east coasts would be the best deterrent against the airships and Zeppelins operating from German North Sea bases. But, of course, as far as these machines were concerned, the British Deperdussin Company was competing for military orders with the very fine waterplanes built by the Short Brothers, who had been in the aeroplane business since February 1909. It is interesting to note that slowly the term 'waterplane' or 'floatplane' was being replaced by 'seaplane' and Winston Churchill, then the First Lord of the Admiralty, was credited with coining the new name in October 1913.

Lieutenant Porte and a small team of mechanics moved onto Osea Island near Millbeach in July. It is presumed that Osea was chosen because of its remoteness; it was situated in mid-stream, surrounded by water for most of the day with access by a causeway at low tide and it was also blessed with several sloping sandy beaches which were ideal for seaplane trials. The two-man crew of the *Seagull* sat in tandem with the observer in the front seat.

The various trials conducted at Osea during July and early August were most unsatisfactory; it seems unlikely that the seaplane ever achieved any flights of more than 50 yards, and certainly it was damaged on several occasions. The single float was replaced with twin main floats as well as wing-tip floats but without much improvement in performance. By August, because of the lack of success the two machines ordered by the Admiralty were cancelled. The company went into liquidation on 23rd August, partly as a result of the failure of the *Seagull* design, but mainly because of the conviction of Monsieur Deperdussin for fraud. However, a British Deperdussin landplane, similar to the *Seagull*, was impressed by the Admiralty (Official No. 885) in August 1914.

In the summer of 1913 two leading aviation personalities, who had first met in Essex, became involved in a rather remarkable wager. Frederick Handley Page and Noel Pemberton Billing met again at Hendon, where Handley Page had been extolling the wonderful flying qualities of his *Yellow Peril* monoplane, which he insisted was so stable that anyone could learn to fly it within 24 hours. Pemberton Billing countered with the opinion that stability did not matter and added, 'Any man who had enough sense to come out of the wet could learn to fly *any* known flying machine in one summer's day'. Handley Page argued that such an assertion was 'utter rubbish'. Whereupon Pemberton Billing maintained that not only could he learn to fly in 24 hours but also obtain his R.Ae.C. certificate in a day. He also issued a challenge to Handley Page to compete with him for a wager of £500; rather rashly, considering his lack of ability as a pilot, Handley Page accepted the bet.

Of course neither man was a complete novice but their attempts at flying had taken place over four years earlier. The date of the challenge was set for 16th September. Pemberton Billing approached several flying training contacts at Brooklands, which was where his brother Eardley and his wife ran the famous Blue Bird restaurant. Harold Barnwell, the Chief Instructor of the Vickers Flying School at Brooklands, agreed to give him instruction but was not prepared to risk one of his school's machines. Whereupon Pemberton Billing bought an old Farman training monoplane from another Brooklands flying school. At a quarter to six on the morning of the appointed day Pemberton Billing started his instruction and in less than three-and-a-half hours had completed all the necessary tests to satisfy the Royal Aero Club's official observer and was awarded his certificate – No. 623!

All this had been accomplished before Handley Page had even begun at Hendon. Barnwell later admitted that Pemberton Billing had shown great aptitude for flying but added, 'if he thinks he knows anything about flying – God help him'! Handley Page accepted defeat graciously and handed over £500; this sum of money helped to finance Pemberton Billing's re-emergence into the world of aviation. His first small flying boat, P.B.1, was placed on display in March 1914 under 'Supermarine (flying lifeboat)' – a name which would be forever linked with the legendary Spitfire fighter of the Second World War.

In April 1914 Clacton-on-Sea was the scene of an 'aviation incident' that made headlines in the national press. In the afternoon of 24th April Winston Churchill was travelling as an official passenger in a Naval Short seaplane from the air station at the Isle of Grain to another air station at Felixstowe. Churchill was the most ardent and active supporter of military aviation then serving in the Government. He took a close personal interest in all aspects of naval aviation, from its aeroplanes and seaplanes, to flying training, tactics and even the planning and siting of seaplane stations. He flew whenever he could despite the unease expressed by his wife, friends and close colleagues. Churchill had also received flying tuition from several naval instructors but, despite completing 24 hours of instruction, he was forbidden to fly solo because of his 'exalted' position as First Sea Lord. In 1943 Churchill would finally be awarded the coveted RAF wings, only the second person (King George V was the first) to receive this honour without having undertaken all the necessary tuition.

The Short S.74 piloted by Lieutenant J. Wilfred Seddon, R.N., experienced a problem with its 160 h.p. Gnôme engine whilst flying along the Essex coast. For safety, Seddon decided to attempt a landing close to a town and he brought the seaplane down on the sea near to Clacton Jetty along the West Beach. Whilst Seddon rang his

The crowd gathered to see Winston Churchill at Clacton-on-Sea in April 1914.

home station for a replacement seaplane, Churchill walked to the Royal Hotel where he remained for a couple of hours until he was recognised by a local journalist who had also served in the Boer War.

Almost immediately the news of the important visitor spread quickly through the town; crowds gathered around the jetty to catch a sight of the famous soldier and politician. According to *The Times*: 'whilst the First Lord was waiting for the replacement machine he was approached by the local militant suffragists...some of their literature was later found in the abandoned seaplane when it was towed that evening into Harwich harbour by the local lifeboat, *Albert Edward*'. Churchill was also reported, in reply to a question from 'a bystander', to have said that 'he considered it part of his duty to understand flying and to visit all the great naval air stations by means of naval seaplanes'. Another Short seaplane (No 19) arrived from Felixstowe and Churchill was able to continue his journey.

It is quite remarkable that neither seaplane survived very long in the Service: No 19 was wrecked at Felixstowe on 15th December

Short S.54 seaplane, 'No 19', arrived at Clacton-on-Sea to collect Winston Churchill.

1914, whereas No 79 was lost at sea on 1st January 1915 but its two-man crew, Lieutenants H.A. Busk and L.H. Strain, were both rescued.

Later in the year the River Crouch was used to trial a locally built 'waterplane'. Two boat-builders at Fambridge, J.J. Talbot and W.B. Quick, had designed a waterplane, which they had patented, No 6829, in 1913. They employed Albert Pink, an engineer from London, to help with the construction work, which was undertaken

Talbot and Quick's waterplane in the Crouch, August 1914.

in one of the disused aeroplane sheds left by Pemberton Billing at South Fambridge. Few details of their machine have survived, except the comment that 'it was of a crude design'. When it was finally launched on the Crouch on 20th August 1914 one of the helpers at the launch was tragically killed. The waterplane travelled for about three hundred yards along the river before it capsized and sank. It certainly never became airborne and nothing more was heard of the machine. But one can only wonder whether Messrs Talbot and Quick were aware that all private flying had been strictly prohibited since 4th August. Now the country was at war with Germany and more serious events were in store for aviation and all those brave and intrepid airmen flying from the numerous landing grounds that suddenly mushroomed throughout Essex.

Chapter 5

Bentfield 'Benny' Hucks

During the immediate pre-war years there was an Essex-born aviator who became a household name throughout the country on account of his fine and spectacular displays of aerobatic flying. Without a shadow of doubt, Bentfield Charles Hucks, or 'Benny' as he was known to his fellow aviators and the public at large, was the most celebrated pioneer aviator to have been born in Essex.

He really deserves far greater honour and acclaim than has hitherto been accorded him in his home county. Benny Hucks did an immense amount to popularise flying in those heady pioneering years and he was the first Essex man to be awarded the coveted R.Ae.C.'s aviator's certificate. His achievements in his relatively short life certainly deserve a separate chapter in a work devoted to early aviation in the county.

Hucks was born at Bentfield End close to Stansted Mountfichet on 25th October 1884, presumably the reason for his unusual christian name. The son of a consultant engineer, it was not too

Bentfield C. Hucks.

surprising that he also trained as an engineer, latterly it is believed with Thorneycrofts. These were exciting days for young engineers, with the rapid rise and development of the motor-car and Hucks entered enthusiastically into this new world. Perhaps it might be said that he was a little too enthusiastic as a motorist because he was 'fined £50 for fast driving' and his licence was suspended for three years! Although it is known that he applied to the Hon. Charles S. Rolls for a position as motor engineer shortly before Rolls was killed in a flying accident, it was the stories of Wilbur Wright's flying exploits in France during 1909 and Louis Blériot's successful crossing of the English Channel in July of that year that fired his determination and resolution to become involved in the 'flying scene', with the ultimate ambition of learning to fly.

Claude Grahame-White recruited several mechanics to support him during his epic London to Manchester flight, and one of them was Hucks; he had promised Hucks that he would teach him to fly. In early August he was with Grahame-White at the air-meeting held at Squires Gate, Blackpool where he met most of the British pioneer aviators including A.V. Roe and Robert Blackburn.

It was at this meeting that Grahame-White and Roe were invited to compete in the Harvard-Boston 'Aero Meet' in America. When Grahame-White set sail for America in the autumn, Hucks accompanied him, along with Reginald Carr and Alfred Turner as his mechanics. It was said that Hucks 'taught himself to fly in 1910' and this was most likely on Grahame-White's Farman; his fellow mechanic, Carr, also became a well-known pilot. The experience he gained in America whilst working for such a superb airman and consummate showman and publicist, must have been invaluable for Hucks and it would have a considerable influence on his future aviation career.

Early in 1911 Hucks was appointed as test pilot for Robert Blackburn, although as yet Hucks had not gained his R.Ae.C.'s aviator's certificate. The two men had first met at the Blackpool air-meeting. They were virtually the same age, from similar backgrounds – engineer fathers and Blackburn had gained a first class honours degree in engineering from Leeds University – and subsequently they became close friends. Hucks received the princely sum of £3 per week, free board and lodgings and commission on sales.

Blackburn had designed and built his first aeroplane in a small workshop in Clifton Street, Leeds, and had tried unsuccessfully to get it airborne from the beach at Marske-by-the-Sea along the Yorkshire coast. Like Handley Page, Bob Blackburn had quickly realised that his talents lay in designing and building aeroplanes rather than flying them, hence his approach to Hucks, although both men shared test flying until Blackburn realised that Hucks was a far better pilot.

Blackburn's second monoplane was taken to a large shed on Filey Cliffs where a concrete slipway was constructed down to the beach and Blackburn also had built a wooden bungalow for the use of his workmen and pilots. It would be trialled from the beach and on 8th March, Hucks managed to get airborne, but he crashed whilst landing as he tried to avoid the cliffs at Filey Briggs; fortunately

Hucks in Blackburn's monoplane at Filey Beach in 1911.

there was no serious damage to either him or the monoplane and he was back flying within a few weeks. Hucks later successfully accomplished a night flight of some sixteen miles from Filey to Scarborough and back.

On 18th May 1911 Hucks passed all the flying tests at Filey Sands but for some reason he was compelled to undergo another flying test before he duly obtained his aviator's certificate, No 91, which was dated 30th May 1911. Blackburn also founded a flying school at Filey where Hucks and Hubert Oxley (the second test pilot) acted as flying instructors.

It was during the summer of 1911 that 'Benny' Hucks became known to a wider audience than the relatively small and enclosed world of British aviation. In July he, along with another twenty airmen, many of them British, took part in the *Daily Mail*'s 'Circuit of Britain Race' for a prize of £10,000. Blackburn had entered two monoplanes, which were named *Mercury*. The race started and finished from Brooklands, but on the second stage from Hendon to Newcastle his *Mercury* crashed six miles north of Luton in Bedfordshire. The prizes were won by two French airmen; 'Colonel' Cody's aeroplane was the only British machine to complete the race.

Later in the summer Hucks flew the repaired *Mercury* on an extended promotional tour of the West Country as publicity for Blackburn Aeroplane Company. The tour, which started on August Bank Holiday at Taunton, lasted three months, during which time he gave numerous flying exhibitions at Burnham, Minehead, Weston-super-Mare, Newport, Cardiff, Cheltenham and Gloucester, and involved a double aerial crossing of the Bristol Channel; he thus became the first aviator to complete the crossing. On 23rd September over Cardiff, Hucks took part in the first ground-to-air wireless telegraphy experiments conducted by H. Grindell Matthews ('the inventor of the new system of wireless telegraphy everyone is talking about'). *The Aeroplane* of 2nd November 1911 commented on his flying tour: 'the whole performance reflects great credit to Mr. Hucks as an aviator and the

Hucks over Burnham in the summer of 1911.

general excellence of the Blackburn monoplane.' In 1912 he wrote a small booklet as publicity material for the Blackburn aeroplane entitled *The Aerial Tourist: What a well designed British built monoplane will stand.*

In 1912 Hucks left Blackburn's and rejoined his old boss and mentor, Claude Grahame-White at his London Aerodrome, Hendon where he was one of the several 'staff' pilots employed by Grahame-White Aviation Company Ltd. According to Grahame-White, Hucks was an excellent 'demonstration pilot'. The Easter meeting held on 5th April was attended by crowds of over 15,000 and Hucks was one of the pilots giving exhibition flights at the meeting. His innate skill as a pilot was fully recognised by Grahame-White and Hucks frequently flew alongside him during his various exhibitions, perhaps most notably in May over the Fleet gathered in Portland Bay for the Royal Review. Also during May, Hucks flew the first airmail service from Hendon to Bath in a Blériot, a distance of about one hundred miles; he carried letters from the Lord Mayor of London to his counterpart in Bath.

On 8th June Hucks, along with other noted British aviators – Samuel Cody, Gustav Hamel, Thomas Sopwith *et al* – took part in the first 'Aerial Derby' staged at Hendon. The 81-mile course was a circuit of London with six turning points including one at Epping. To my knowledge this was the first time that Hucks had flown over his home county. Nevertheless, two weeks later he was back in Essex to attend Grahame-White's wedding at Hylands House where he flew over Widford church dropping confetti on the bridal party.

For the next two months Hucks was engaged on Grahame-White's 'Wake Up, England' tour. He was allocated towns in the Midlands and Yorkshire at which to give flying exhibitions. Hucks was approached by a rich, colonial sportsman, Harold Barlow, who had grandiose plans to organise flying tours of Australia and his native New Zealand. It is reputed that Barlow paid Grahame-White £1,000 to release Hucks from his contract with the Grahame-White Aviation Company Ltd. Hucks accompanied Barlow to France to test a Blériot – an X1-2 – a two-seater to carry a passenger, which Barlow purchased and Hucks flew back to England. Because of ill-health Barlow's Australian plans were

Hucks in his Blériot during the 'Wake Up England' tour.

placed on hold but Hucks took the Blériot, now named *Firefly*, on a tour of England and Scotland giving flying displays, which were sponsored by the *Daily Mail*.

Sadly, in January 1913 Barlow died, but because of his fast-growing popularity Hucks decided to branch out on his own. He formed his own company, which had its offices at 100 Piccadilly, London, and he purchased *Firefly* from the Barlow estate. Like Grahame-White, he also employed a 'business manager', J.C. Savage, another ex-mechanic of Grahame-White's; after the Great War, Savage pioneered the art of 'sky writing' – aerial advertising. Hucks had 'B.C. Hucks' boldly emblazoned on the underside of each wing, although the public knew him as 'Benny' Hucks; he now undertook a long and exhausting country-wide tour giving exhibitions, competing in races and carrying passengers. It was estimated that he gave over 2,000 people their first experience of flying. Whilst he was touring Scotland he was given a Royal Command by King George V to fly to Balmoral and land on the

Hucks, in the centre, during one of his flying exhibition tours.

The CAMP GROUND
(Cricket Field Lane, Near Station),
SKEGNESS.
AUGUST 19th, 20th, and 21st.

B. C. HUCKS

THE FAMOUS AIRMAN,
WILL GIVE THRILLING

Demonstrations
of Flying = =

In his new 80 h.p. BLERIOT
MONOPLANE.

**Flights at frequent intervals
between 2.30 and 4.30 p.m.,
and 6 p.m. till dusk.**

PASSENGERS Carried Daily.

For full particulars apply the Hon Sec —
MR. G. G DUNKLEY, Boston House, Lumley Road, Skegness.

"News" Office, Skegness.

Poster advertising B.C. Hucks – 'The Famous Airman'.

Castle grounds but unfortunately the winds were too strong to accomplish this.

Besides his exhibition flying and passenger flights, Hucks put his aeroplane to other uses. In 1912 he was engaged in electioneering in Midlothian, canvassing by air for one of the candidates. Later at Newcastle-upon-Tyne he carried out deliveries of tobacco for a tobacco firm. Hucks also made news on the ground; he went on a lecture tour during the winter months when he spoke about his 'Three Years' Experience of Flying'. In June 1913 he returned to Essex to give a flying display at Loxford Park, Ilford, and the following year he appeared at Barking.

In September 1913 a young French pilot, Celestin-Adolphe Pegoud, astonished crowds at Brooklands with 'a most remarkable display of aerobatics including "looping-the-loop" or quite literally flying on his head', as one newspaper reported. Hucks went to France where he was taught to loop-the-loop by Pegoud and on 1st November he became the first British pilot to achieve it in his specially-built Blériot X1 at Hendon in front of a large crowd of over 50,000 spectators. He immediately became the toast of London.

Later another celebrated Hendon pilot and close friend, Gustav Hamel, also looped-the-loop. On 16th January 1914, to celebrate the event, Hucks and Hamel were the honoured guests at an 'upside-down' dinner held at the Royal Aero Club in London, which had been organised by Grahame-White. The tables were suspended from the ceiling and the food was served back to front, starting with coffee and ending with soup! The Directors of the London Aerodrome presented Hucks with a Gold Medal to mark his first 'loop-the-loop'. When RAF Hendon closed down in 1987 an 'Upside-Down' dinner was held in the Officers' Mess to commemorate the first dinner some sixty years earlier.

By 1914 Hucks had three Blériots, two single-seaters and a two-seater for passengers. He had teamed up with Marcus 'Boy' Manton, another Hendon staff pilot, who at the age of 18 had been the youngest airman to gain his aviator's certificate. They proceeded to thrill thousands of people around the country with their daring and spectacular flying displays, which include switch-backs', 'spiral vol-planes', 'upside-down flying' and, of course, looping-the-loop; by May it was said that Hucks had completed more than 400, his record then being 13 continuous loops. The sudden and tragic death of Gustav Hamel in May (he disappeared without trace whilst crossing the English Channel) made Hucks, without a shadow of doubt, the most celebrated and brilliant aerobatic pilot in the country.

During the summer of 1914 he and Manton made an extensive tour of the West Country and the Midlands but, in June, Hucks returned to Essex to appear at the Essex County Show held at Waltham Abbey. On this occasion Hucks had to obtain special permission from the War Office because a strict embargo had been introduced on aeroplanes flying over or near to military installations; there was a large munitions factory at Waltham Abbey.

At the outbreak of war Hucks, like so many of his aviation colleagues, joined the Royal Flying Corps. His three Blériots were requisitioned and one was immediately returned to him to fly as a military pilot! In September 1914 2nd Lieutenant Hucks was sent up to the Lake District. There had been persistent rumours that a German Zeppelin was hiding somewhere in the valleys, which according to many locals came out at night to reconnoitre the area! It is perhaps needless to say that Hucks did not find any signs of the 'ghost' Zeppelin.

Hucks was involved in ferrying aeroplanes out to France and is believed to have seen active service, flying B.E.2 scouts with No 4 Squadron. He was later invalided home with severe pleurisy. But now, at the rank of Captain in the R.F.C. Reserve, he perhaps found his true forte – as a test pilot with Ruston and Proctor. His flying prowess was greatly appreciated by Geoffrey de Havilland, the Chief Designer *and* test pilot of the Aircraft Manufacturing Company (A.M.C., but later more generally known as AIRCO).

Because de Havilland had found that combining the two tasks was too onerous, he offered Hucks the post of Chief Test Pilot; so Hucks now found himself back in very familiar surroundings at Hendon. Grahame-White's aerodrome had been requisitioned by the military authorities.

As de Havilland remarked about Hucks: 'as a test and demonstration pilot he was outstanding, far better than I was [fulsome praise from a fine pilot]…he was a most modest and very likeable man'. During the height of his popularity Hucks was a very retiring and unassuming person, who tried to eschew publicity and always referred to himself as plain 'B.C. or Ben'. Some of the famous aeroplanes Hucks first flew and tested at Hendon were the D.H.4 in November 1916, the D.H. 9a and the D.H.10 Mk11, a twin-engine bomber, in March 1917.

It was during his time with A.M.C. that Hucks' inventive talents came to the fore, most notably with his so-styled 'Hucks mobile starter'. In those days aero-engines had to be started by the rather dangerous method of swinging the propeller, which had led to several fatalities and numerous serious injuries. Hucks developed a basic Ford Model 'T' chassis and engine which he adapted to drive a long horizontal shaft that enabled the aero-engine to be started, at which stage it automatically disengaged. The self-starter became an instant success and it was immediately ordered by the Air Ministry and soon every R.F.C. aerodrome was supplied with a 'Hucks Starter'. Thus his name and fame were perpetuated in what became the Royal Air Force long after his death.

Hucks' lack of celebrity in his home county may be due in some part to his early and untimely death. The influenza pandemic of 1918 claimed his life; he died of pneumonia on 6th November aged only 34, just five days before the end of the First World War. According to the Commonwealth War Graves Commission, Captain Bentfield Charles Hucks is buried in Grave 39669 in Highgate Cemetery, London.

Chapter 6

Essex Landing Grounds and their Aircraft during the Great War (1914–1918)

On 4th August 1914 Great Britain declared war on Germany and the Home Secretary issued an order 'prohibiting the navigation of aircraft of every class and description over the whole area of the United Kingdom and the whole of the coastline and territorial waters thereto adjacent'. For the next six years the only aeroplanes to be seen in the skies above Essex were either British military aircraft or those belonging to the enemy, and more often their dreaded airships.

The Government had decided that the Royal Naval Air Service (R.N.A.S.) would be responsible for the country's air defence until such time as the R.F.C. had trained a sufficient number of pilots to take over 'Home Defence' duties. Lord Kitchener, the Secretary of State for War, signed the necessary decree on 2nd September. However, Winston Churchill, as First Lord of the Admiralty, warned 'the Admiralty could not be responsible for Home Defence but could only be responsible for doing the best possible with the material available'.

In fact the R.N.A.S. had only been formally created on 1st July out of the existing Naval Wing of the Corps, some R.F.C. officers jokingly referring to the new Service as 'Really Not A Sailor'! It was even more inadequately prepared and equipped than the R.F.C., with a total of about ninety land and seaplanes of which maybe fifty could be considered ready for operations, and some of these had already been sent to operate from bases in France.

As the counties of East Anglia and Kent were in the direct path of any airships bound for London, it became imperative to set up landing grounds close to and to the east of London as well as providing additional seaplane bases along those coasts. Thus, by the end of 1914, six landing grounds and a seaplane station had been sited in Essex.

Actually on 2nd August a new R.N.A.S. 'sub-station' was formed at Clacton-on-Sea. Three Short Type 74 tractor seaplanes arrived from R.N.A.S. Grain, in Kent, to alight on the West Beach along Marine Parade from where they would operate; the nearby Martello Tower was used as the Station headquarters. These seaplanes were the first military aircraft to be based in Essex. They had first entered the Naval Wing in January 1914 and ultimately twelve served in the R.N.A.S. The two-man crews were required to patrol the Thames Estuary regularly but, as the seaplanes were unarmed, if the crews sighted an enemy aircraft or airship they used very basic wireless/telegraphy equipment to report to either Grain or Eastchurch where armed landplanes were based. In December another two seaplanes were allocated to Clacton and they remained there until the sub-station was closed down during the autumn of 1916.

One of the first military aircraft to be based in Essex.

In October the first R.N.A.S. landing ground in Essex opened at Hainault Farm, where about sixty acres bordered by the Hainault and Forest Roads had been requisitioned. In the same month some twenty acres of farmland alongside Lower Ford Lane, Writtle near Chelmsford were levelled and prepared to provide a temporary landing ground for the use of the R.F.C. It had been decided that a few aircraft could be spared from its No 1 Reserve Squadron, based at Farnborough, to assist the meagre Home Defence forces. The first two aircraft, a B.E.2b and a Maurice Farman Longhorn, did not appear until mid-December and they began patrolling over the Christmas period. Writtle was never a very active landing ground and closed down in November 1916.

Another R.F.C. landing ground came into use in the autumn; it was situated to the south of Rochford and the river Roach, bordered in the south by Eastwoodbury Lane close to Warners Bridge. Although named Rochford, it was also known as Eastwood. It was originally intended to provide flying training for R.F.C. airmen but was later developed into the most extensive flying ground in Essex (some one hundred and sixty acres) with the largest number of squadrons and units based there. In 1918 Cecil Lewis, of *Sagittarius Rising* fame, was posted to 61 Squadron at Rochford and described it as 'a magnificent aerodrome almost a mile square'. It then had two separate sites – operational and flying training – one to the west of the ground close to Westbarrow Hall and the other in the south alongside Eastwoodbury Lane.

Towards the end of 1914 the largest R.N.A.S. station in Essex opened at Chingford. An area of land (150 acres) to the west of the town towards Potters Bar and almost on the county boundary with Middlesex was developed into a 'Branch Station'. The first aircraft to arrive were four Bristol T.B.8s and their crews immediately began 'airship patrols'. These two-seater biplanes had first flown in August 1913 and had been designed by Bristol & Colonial Aeroplane Company's chief designer – Henri Coanda, a Rumanian engineer; the company used *Bristol* as a trademark. The T.B.8 cruised at 65 to 75 m.p.h. depending on the size of their Le Rhône engines and had an endurance of five hours; it was the company's first successful aeroplane and 53 were built for the R.N.A.S.

Also during December, two other R.N.A.S. Branch Stations opened, one at Burnham-on-Crouch and the other at Widford,

Bristol T.B.8s first arrived at R.N.A.S. Chingford in late 1914.

Blackburn's A.D. Sparrow or Scout, 'No 1536', at Chingford. (Imperial War Museum)

close to Chelmsford. The landing ground at Burnham-on-Crouch was situated about a mile to the east of the town and ran due north from Burnham Wick. Widford (always referred to as Chelmsford) was a rather small ground of 22 acres situated to the north-east of Widford Hall Lane. The landing ground was barely a stone's throw from the church where Grahame-White had been married two years earlier. Like Chingford, both stations were supplied with two T.B.8s.

In early 1915 Chingford received four rare aeroplanes. The A.D. Sparrow or Scout was a single-seat pusher biplane designed by Harris Booth of the Admiralty's Design Section specifically for 'anti-airship patrols'. It was powered by an 80 h.p. Gnôme engine, giving it a top speed of 84 m.p.h. and an endurance of some two-and-a-half hours. The Scout was a rather strange and cumbersome machine that proved to be too heavy, underpowered and difficult to control in the air. As with several other aircraft designed and built during the early years of the war, the A.D Scout was a failure and only four were built.

The Admiralty decided to change Chingford from an operational station to a flying training depot to provide preliminary flying instruction. After a spell of basic training at Crystal Palace, R.N.A.S. airmen arrived at Chingford to begin their flying training, where they completed about twenty or so hours' solo flying before passing into Cranwell for advanced flying instruction. Several well-known First World War airmen served at Chingford as flying instructors – Warren Merriam, a pre-war Brooklands instructor, Hubert Broad, who later became de Havilland's Chief Test Pilot and Ben Travers, perhaps better known as a successful playwright. He served at Chingford during 1916 and described the landing ground as 'a strip of fogbound and soggy meadowland at Ponders End between a reservoir and a sewage farm'!

Various machines were used for flying training, perhaps most notably the T.B.8s, but in the early days the Depot was supplied with a couple of Avro 503s, one of the predecessors of A.V Roe & Co's most successful 504 series of aircraft. It was a two-seater biplane which had originally been constructed as a seaplane; strangely the prototype had been sold in June 1913 to the German Navy. At the request of the R.N.A.S. the other three 503s were converted to landplanes and one of these, No 51, crashed on the banks of the nearby King George Reservoir on 8th August 1915 when being flown by Flight Sub-Lieutenant Norman Blackburn (of the famous aeroplane company) and was withdrawn from service. Chingford remained a major R.N.A.S. training depot until April 1918 when it was taken over by the newly formed Royal Air Force. It then became a Mobilisation Station for three R.A.F. squadrons that were formed there during the year.

The arrival of the first two Zeppelins over Norfolk on the evening of 19th January 1915 heralded what later became known as 'the year of the Zeppelin', when in ten night raids considerable bomb damage was sustained as well as a number of civilian deaths and injuries. These airship raids clearly showed the woeful and inadequate state of the country's Home Defence and during the next two years over twenty landing grounds were opened in Essex, four of which – Goldhanger, Sutton's Farm, North Weald Bassett and Stow Maries – became Flight Stations and were heavily engaged in

S.E.5A: a rugged and reliable fighter arrived in the spring of 1917.

the desperate battle against German airships. These stations, as their name implies, permanently housed a Flight of six aircraft.

During March 1915 the sites for two emergency night landing grounds were selected by the War Office for use by the R.F.C. There

Avro 503, 'No 51', crashed near Chingford on 8th August 1915. (R.A.F. Museum)

had been growing concern that the relatively few R.F.C. aircraft flying night patrols around London might require such grounds in the case of engine failure (a fairly frequent occurrence in those days), shortage of fuel or even battle damage. One of these grounds was sited at Blackheath Common about two miles to the south of Colchester along the Mersea road. The other ground was about one-and-a-half miles to the west of Horndon-on-the-Hill and really closer to Orsett than Horndon.

The landing grounds were placed in one of three classifications. Those designated First Class were require to have no natural or man-made restrictions that might endanger aeroplane landings from any direction. Second Class grounds had either buildings and/or trees which might be hazardous to landings in one direction, whereas Third Class grounds had landing hazards in more than one direction. To be selected as a Flight Station the landing ground had to satisfy all the criteria for a First Class ground and preferably be near to a railway station for ease of the supply of stores and as a useful aid to aerial navigation.

From April 1915 Chingford, as befitted its new training role, was rapidly developed to accommodate all the trainee airmen and their flying instructors. At the same time the R.N.A.S. relinquished the control of the landing ground at Hainault Farm and it was passed over to the R.F.C. for use as a night-landing ground. Later in the year the War Office acquired some additional land which increased the flying ground to 100 acres. Ultimately Hainault Farm would be provided with the usual range of buildings and facilities – stores, workshops, 'aeroplane sheds', motor transport sheds, armoury, bomb stores, guard room, reception station, barrack blocks and officers' mess and quarters – that were essential to operate as a First Class Flight Station. Meanwhile the R.N.A.S. had acquired an additional landing ground at Fairlop which was virtually the same site (although larger in area) as used by Handley Page in 1911/1912. Fairlop remained as a flying training depot until April 1919. It was only about half a mile from the R.F.C.'s Flight Station at Hainault Farm.

Caudron G3s were based at Widford and Burnham-on-Crouch. (R.A.F. Museum)

Both Widford and Burnham-on-Crouch night-landing grounds remained under Naval control until 1916. Widford, along with Chingford, was provided with a basic flare path to aid night landings in March 1915 and was supplied with three new aircraft – Caudron G.3s. These were French-built biplanes and looked rather flimsy and ungainly; they were powered by Anzani engines and had a top speed of 70 m.p.h; subsequently they proved unsuitable for night patrols and were relegated to training duties. The Widford landing ground closed down in the following September, whereas Burnham-on-Crouch was taken over by the R.F.C. in April 1916.

Some seventy acres of land, largely comprised of Gardener's Farm at Goldhanger, was requisitioned to provide the R.N.A.S. with an advance night landing ground. The site lay to the south of the Maldon Road running down to the river Blackwater and, unusually, Gardener's Farm was almost in the centre of the landing field. Goldhanger opened in August but was barely used until it was passed over to the R.F.C. in the following April when it was provided with accommodation, workshops and four large aeroplane sheds. The first operational aircraft did not arrive until September when it was designated a R.F.C. Flight Station.

On the night of 31st May/1st June, one Zeppelin reached London and the capital was bombed for the first time. Further

B.E.2cs were the most successful against the Zeppelins. (via G. Weir)

airship raids continued until mid-October and they created indignation in the country; the Government was criticised in Parliament and in the Press for failing to protect the country against such attacks. It was decided to place the control of Home Defence under the War Office and transfer the responsibility for Home Defence duties to the R.F.C. However, the Corps was faced by an almost insatiable demand for aircraft and pilots to serve in France and it was recognised that the formal handover would not be able to take place until early 1916; the actual date was 10th February.

During the summer of 1915 another area of farmland (90 acres) was requisitioned at Sutton's Farm near the village of Hornchurch (the location was officially stated as '2 miles WSW of Hornchurch') to become the R.F.C.'s No 11 Landing Ground. Sutton's Farm officially opened on 3rd October when two B.E.2c biplanes of No 13 Squadron, then based at Gosport, Hampshire, arrived to join a ground party of a dozen airmen at No 23 Squadron. A few days later another three pilots arrived. At the same time two B.E.2c biplanes were sent to Hainault Farm, now known as No 111 Landing Ground. Like most landing grounds the facilities at Sutton's Farm were rather basic but during 1916 all the necessary support buildings and accommodation were erected at the north-eastern corner of the flying ground and to the south of the farmhouse.

In 1916 no less than sixteen landing grounds opened in the county, including two famous Flight Stations at North Weald Bassett and Stow Maries. North Weald Bassett, which was sited to the north-west of the village and bordered in the south by the Epping road, opened in April, whereas Stow Maries did not open until mid-September. It was situated some three-quarters of a mile north-west of the village and subsequently the station's buildings were placed in the south-west corner of the ground alongside Strawberry Hill.

During the year various R.F.C. emergency night-landing grounds were established at Beaumont, Broomfield Court, Chelmsford, East Hanningfield, Easthorpe, Fyfield, Little Clacton, Mountnessing, North Benfleet, North Ockendon, Orsett, Shenfield, Sible Hedingham and Wormingford. Some of these grounds were only open for a short duration. Beaumont, for instance, operated from April to August; it was replaced by the new landing ground at Plough Corner, Little Clacton which opened in October. The small ground at Mountnessing (only 21 acres) was established in April only to be closed in December when a larger landing ground at Palmers Farm at Shenfield had opened in September. East Hanningfield, half a mile to the west of the village, was set up in April but closed at the end of the year as the Flight Station at Stow Maries was only three miles away. North Ockendon survived from April to October, when it had become superfluous with the opening of Orsett in October. Given its position to the south of the old A13 road and to the south-west of the Cock Inn, and in flat open land with no natural encumbrances, Orsett was one of the few emergency landing grounds to be designated First Class.

Each night-landing ground was allocated to one of the Home Defence squadrons operating from the Flight Stations, but they were, of course, available for any emergency landings. The majority of these grounds did not see any landings throughout their existence. No permanent accommodation was provided, merely a number of tents for the small detachment of men of the Royal Defence Corps who maintained the very basic lighting system – just three flares. Nevertheless, even as late as March 1918 there is a report that German prisoners of war were 'working on' the landing ground at Broomfield Court near Chelmsford.

The final three night-landing grounds opened in 1917: Braintree Green and Thaxted in January, then Runwell later in August. Thaxted was the only landing ground in the county that was allocated to a Squadron – No 75 – based outside Essex; its first Commander was Major Henry A. Petre, D.S.O., and M.C. After his brother's death in December 1912 Henry had arrived in Australia in the following January, where he helped to found a military flying school at Point Clear near Melbourne and the Australian Flying Corps. Petre's youngest brother, John or 'Jack', was the third of the Petre brothers to become an aviator. He had joined the R.N.A.S and, as a Squadron Commander, he was killed in action in April 1917.

One small day-landing ground, situated at Silchester Corner, Bournes Green, was used briefly during May 1917. It housed a number of R.F.C. aircraft that pulled targets for ground-to-air firing practice for the artillery ranges at Shoeburyness. After less than a month the ground was closed when it was recognised that such firing practice posed a danger to the nearby built-up areas of Thorpe Bay and Shoeburyness.

The radical reorganisation of the country's Home Defence had necessitated the formation of new R.F.C. squadrons specially designated for Home Defence duties. The first one to serve in Essex was No 39(HD) at Hainault Farm, which was formed in April 1916 under the command of Major T.C.R. Higgins; moreover it was the first (HD) Squadron to be formed. It comprised three Flights – 'A' to 'C'; 'A' was placed at North Weald Bassett, 'B' at Sutton's Farm, whilst 'C' remained at Hainault Farm. The squadron had its headquarters at Woodford Green. Each flight was equipped with six B.E.2cs. No 39 was the most successful squadron operating in Essex against the German airships; its pilots destroyed four and in each case they were flying B.E.2cs.

The other (HD) Squadron operating in Essex during 1916 was No 37. Since April it had been engaged in an experimental role at Orfordness, in Suffolk, and had reformed at Woodford Green under Major W.B. Hargrave on 15th September, but a fortnight later its headquarters was transferred to Woodham Mortimer. The squadron's 'A' Flight was based at Rochford, 'B' at Stow Maries and 'C' at Goldhanger, and they were provided with a mixture of B.E.2cs and B.E.12s, although mainly the latter.

The B.E.12 appeared in Essex during 1916. (via G. Weir)

The B.E.2 was designed, developed and built by the Royal Aircraft Factory and had first appeared in 1912; B.E. stood for 'Blériot Experimental'. The B.E.2c had first flown in June 1914 and was a most remarkable aircraft, with over 1,300 being produced. It had a maximum speed of 77 m.p.h. although it took 35 minutes to reach an altitude of 10,000 feet. The B.E.2c became the R.F.C.'s all-purpose aircraft, used for reconnaissance, artillery spotting, bombing, training and perhaps most successfully on airship patrols. It gained a reputation of being steady, very reliable and easy to fly, especially at night.

The B.E.12 was a far newer variant, which first appeared in July 1916 and was effectively a higher-powered single-seat B.E.2c. Although the performance of both aircraft proved adequate against the airships, when German heavy bombers – GIVs or 'Gothas' – first appeared over England in May 1917 their shortcomings became rather apparent: a lack of speed, poor rate of climb and general manoeuvrability. They were replaced by the new and faster fighters that had emerged – Bristol F2bs, Sopwith Pups and Camel F1s and S.E.5s.

With the potent threat of the Gothas, several day-fighter squadrons were formed during 1917; the designation (HD) had been dropped in November 1916. The first to be formed in Essex was No 44 at Hainault Farm on 24th July, which was originally placed under the command of Major T.O'B. Hubbard, who coincidentally had acted as the Royal Aero Club's observer when Edward Petre had gained his R.Ae.C. certificate exactly five years previously. He was later replaced by Major G.W. Murliss-Green. The squadron was originally equipped with Sopwith $1\frac{1}{2}$-strutters but within a month they were replaced by Sopwith Camels.

Also during July, No 61 Squadron was formed at Rochford from a nucleus of pilots from 37 Squadron. They received sixteen Sopwith Pups, which were exchanged in December for S.E.5As. Because of the formation of the new squadron, No 37's 'A' Flight was moved to Stow Maries. Nevertheless, 61 Squadron remained at Rochford until it was disbanded in June 1919.

Sopwith Pup at Hainault Farm. (via G. Weir)

One might be forgiven for thinking that the Home Defence force was virtually Sopwith's air force in all but name. Thomas O.M. Sopwith, the famous pre-war aviator, had started aeroplane manufacture at Brooklands in 1912 and the following year he founded the Sopwith Aviation Company. During the war over 12,000 aircraft were built by the company and 30 sub-contractors. Sopwith Dolphins, $1^1/_2$-strutters, Pups, Camels and Snipes all flew from Essex landing grounds over the next three years. Three Sopwith Triplanes were built under contract by Oakley Ltd of Ilford Aeroplane Works, Ilford; they were the only aircraft manufactured in Essex during the war. One has survived (N5912) and is displayed in the R.A.F. Museum at Hendon.

The Sopwith Pup was considered 'a perfect flying machine...with no tricks or vices...it handled like a thoroughbred'. Although over 1,800 Pups were built, its thunder was stolen by its successor – the Camel – which gained its name from the humped top line of its fuselage. It has been immortalised by the famous *Biggles* stories of Captain W.E. Johns. Although the Camel had none of the Pup's docile handling qualities and was not easy to fly, once mastered it was highly manoeuvrable with an impressive performance – top speed 120 m.p.h., and armed with twin Lewis guns firing above the propeller. The Camel was the most successful WW1 fighter, credited with the destruction of more enemy aircraft than any other. Over 5,800 were produced and by the end of 1918 thirty-eight R.A.F. squadrons were equipped with Camels.

The S.E.5A was the product of the Royal Aircraft Factory and had first appeared in November 1916. It was a rugged, reliable and steady fighter armed with two Vickers guns, one sited on the top wing so that its fire was clear of the propeller. With a top speed of 120 m.p.h. and an operational ceiling of 19,500 ft it was an impressive fighter, but perhaps less successful on night operations because of the length of time needed to warm up its Hispano-Suiza engine. S.E.5As first became operational in France with the celebrated 56 Squadron; its 'A' Flight flew briefly from Rochford on Home Defence patrols during June 1917. After the war, many S.E.5As were sold into private hands and they chiefly became known for pioneering skywriting.

During August, No 46 Squadron which had operated from Sutton's Farm since the previous month, was posted back to France and was replaced by No 78 Squadron under Major C.R. Rowden; it was also equipped with Sopwith 1½-strutters but they were soon replaced by Camels. The squadron remained at Sutton's Farm until disbanded in December 1919.

In the same month the two Flights of 39 Squadron, which had been based at Sutton's and Hainault Farms, were moved to North Weald Bassett and in the following month its pilots received another remarkable fighter – the Bristol F.2(b) or 'Brisfit'. It was larger than the Camel and since entering operations with the R.F.C. in France in March, it had gained a fearsome reputation. Twin-armed with a top speed of 117 m.p.h. the F.2(b) could operate up to 18,000 ft.

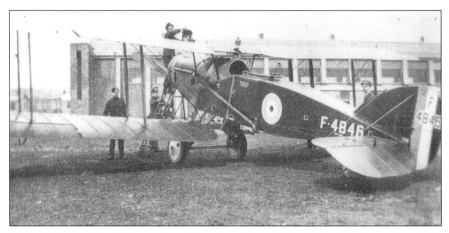

Bristol F.2(b): No 39 Squadron flew them from North Weald Bassett in 1918. (via G. Weir)

Over 7,500 were built and it is perhaps a measure of their 'advanced' design, performance and durability that they remained in service with the R.A.F. until 1932.

As a sign of the growing strength of the R.F.C., several special night-flying training units were set up during 1917/1918, followed by the formation of the first three specialist night-fighter squadrons – Nos 151 to 153 in January 1918. No 141 Squadron was formed in Rochford and placed under the command of Major Philip Babington (later Air Marshal Sir Philip). It was equipped with yet another Sopwith fighter – the Dolphin; within a month it had moved to Biggin Hill. Since January 1917 Rochford had become involved in night-flying training with the arrival of No 11 Reserve (Night Training) Squadron. During its stay at Rochford it underwent several changes of name, ultimately becoming No 198 (Night) Training Squadron. In April 1918 Sutton's Farm also became involved in flying training when No 189 Training Squadron arrived from Yorkshire.

On 10th March 1918 Sopwith's newest fighter, the Snipe, planned as a replacement for the Camel, appeared at Sutton's Farm

Sopwith NF Camel over Sutton's Farm. (via G. Weir)

for a flight demonstration in front of a number of the R.F.C.'s 'top brass'. It was flown by the legendary Captain James McCudden, V.C. It was the last Sopwith fighter to be developed during the war and although an excellent aircraft it arrived too late to see much action; Nos 37, 44 and 61 Squadrons were provided with Snipes during January 1919.

In March 1917 the seventy-one pilots then serving in the Home Defence squadrons were described by one national newspaper as 'a thin line of young men with their flimsy machines bravely and valiantly battling in the night skies against the monstrous Zepps'. Just how well these brave young men contended first with the German airships and later the Gotha bombers in the skies above Essex, is a story of courage and heroism equal to the feats of their colleagues over the trenches in France, which have received far more publicity and greater acclaim.

Chapter 7

When 'Death Rained From The Skies'

Even before the war the public had been gripped with a Zeppelin or 'Zepp' mania, mainly on account of some dire Government propaganda and lurid newspaper articles speculating on the consequences of an aerial bombardment. When war was declared, many people were convinced that 'the peaceful skies over England would be no more'. Such fears were further heightened when, on 26th August 1914, Antwerp was bombed by a Zeppelin; this 'barbarous attack' killed twelve civilians. From then on the 'monstrous Zepps' were expected daily and when they came, 'death rained from the skies'. Winston Churchill had no doubts that 'an aerial attack upon England must be a feature of the near future'.

The introduction of a system of aerial defence around London in September 1914 only added to the public's fear. It comprised a ring

German Navy Zeppelin – 1915 – the 'Dreaded Zepp'.

of gun batteries, searchlights and voluntary observers. Then from 1st October, a total 'black-out' between the hours of 5 p.m. and 7.30 a.m. was imposed in London; street lights were extinguished or shaded and householders were required to draw their blinds before lights were lit. These measures were hugely unpopular, more especially during the winter of 1914 when the expected 'Zepps' did not arrive; many refused to comply with the restrictions claiming that they were 'not afraid of Zeppelins'.

Despite the several landing grounds that had already been established in Essex, even in November 1914 aeroplanes were still a relative novelty in the Essex skies. The Rev. Andrew Clark, Rector of Great Leighs, entered in his diary for 18th November: 'Word was sent from Chelmsford to Great Leighs that aeroplanes would pass over today. The message was sent to prevent the population from panic. There has been so much talk of invasion by German airships. I have not heard that anyone has seen them.'

However, it would not be very long before 'the dreaded Zepps' would appear, to be heard rather than actually seen by the majority of people living in Essex. I well remember being told by a lady in her nineties, who was born in Leigh-on-Sea, that she could not remember seeing her first aeroplane, but she vividly recalled being taken by her father up onto the cliffs to see a Zeppelin pass along the Thames Estuary, it was 'like a gigantic silver cigar'.

During 1915 there were twenty airship raids causing considerable damage and the loss of two hundred lives with over one hundred and fifty injured. The 420 ft long Zeppelins (more later models were even bigger at 520 ft) appeared to be indestructible and roamed high in the night skies with apparent impunity; the distinctive roar of their engines could clearly be heard and soon began 'to instil a special kind of fear'.

They encountered scant opposition from the relatively few R.N.A.S. aircraft. The problems facing these intrepid airmen were formidable. Taking off and landing, especially at night, was extremely hazardous despite the provision of flares. Most of the aircraft were too slow and did not have the climbing speed to counter the Zeppelins. Should they sight an airship their armament

Spital Road, Maldon after the Zeppelin bombing in April 1915.

was woefully inadequate – they were provided with bombs to drop on the airships but incendiary bullets were later introduced. The cockpits of their aeroplanes were not fitted with any instrument lighting and Lieutenant Cecil Lewis later recalled his night patrols as 'two hour stretches of utter frustration, all we could hope to locate was the glow of an exhaust …and then at the end of the patrol, we hoped that by the grace of God we could land safely'.

The first raid on Essex occurred on the evening of 21st February 1915 when a solitary aircraft crossed the coast at Clacton-on-Sea, flew to Braintree and dropped two incendiary bombs before returning by way of Coggeshall and Colchester, where high explosive bombs were dropped, but fortunately no lives were lost. It was thought that the Marconi wireless masts at Chelmsford were the target. In April (15th/16th) Zeppelin L.6, under the command of *Oberleutnant* von Buttlar-Brandenfels, crossed the coast at Landguard Fort near Harwich, where the soldiers opened fire with their rifles. The Zeppelin dropped 34 bombs on Maldon and Heybridge, which damaged a number of properties and one small girl was injured. On the night of 9th/10th May, Zeppelin LZ.38 commanded by *Hauptmann* Erich Linnartz, arrived over Leigh-on-Sea and Southend-on-Sea but was frustrated by gunfire from a battery on Canvey Island. Several bombs were dropped and also 'a calling card' which bore the message: 'You English. We have come and will come again. Kill or cure. German'!

There were widespread rumours of German spies and reports of motor-car lights signalling to the Zeppelins. In August the Rev. Clark noted that 'there was a strong village report that a motor with bright headlights flashed along the Great North Road guiding the Zeppelins. It is difficult to believe these reports, coming independently from different sources, and dovetailing in with each other, are groundless.'

He also reported that five bombs had fallen on Chelmsford during the night of 17th/18th August, one of which 'went through the roof of a house, through a room in which a child was sleeping,

Bomb damage at Braintree on 31st March 1916.

and buried itself in the ground-floor...much damage at Stratford, Leyton and Ilford. Leytonstone station has been flattened and 49 people killed. This news is prohibited because it is within six miles of London and it is not wished that the Germans should know how nearly they had reached the capital.' Certainly on that night two Caudron G.3s were sent up on patrol in an attempt to intercept the solitary Zeppelin (L.10) and both crashed on landing at Widford, their Hale bombs exploded and both pilots were injured.

With so many Zeppelins flying over Essex it was decided, in October, that 'extra special constables' were to be appointed in towns and villages throughout the county; their duty was 'to warn the inhabitants that Zeppelins were on hand. These "extra specials" are to have long poles, with pads on the end, to reach up and rap upon upper-storey windows to warn about lights'. Although many felt that this was 'absolute folly because the first action of every sleeper so aroused will be to light gas or candle and every street will be alight in a moment'.

Because of the several raids on London the Lord Mayor, Sir Charles Wakefield, offered a prize of £500 to the first person or persons to destroy a Zeppelin over the British Isles. As yet no single pilot had managed to sight, let alone intercept a Zeppelin, but the various gun batteries around the county had frequently been in action; many were manned by companies of the Essex and Suffolk Royal Garrison Artillery (E.&S.R.G.A.).

On 13th October an airman from Sutton's Farm became the first R.F.C. pilot to locate a Zeppelin: Second Lieutenant John C. Slessor of 23 Squadron was engaged in his first night patrol in a B.E.2c, when he sighted Zeppelin L.15, which had been caught in searchlight beams high over Romford. It had already successfully bombed London causing considerable damage and the deaths of 72 civilians and injuring another 120. By the time Slessor had made his slow climb through thick cloud, L.15 had long made its escape. Slessor managed to land back at Sutton's Farm in foggy conditions but heavily damaged the undercarriage of his aeroplane in the process, although he escaped injury. He later had an outstanding R.A.F. career during the Second World War and was the Chief of the Air Staff from 1950 to 1952.

The same Zeppelin, still commanded by *Kapitän-Leutnant* Breithaupt, was the first to be destroyed over Essex by the combined efforts of the gun batteries and a R.F.C. airman. On the night of 31st March/1st April 1916 four Naval Zeppelins (L13/14/15/16) were in action. L.14, commanded by *Kapitän* Böcker, bombed Sudbury in Suffolk and then dropped three bombs on Braintree, which damaged some houses in Coronation Street and left four people dead. It also bombed Chelmsford and the oil refineries at Thameshaven and, despite coming under fire from several gun batteries, L.14 escaped across the North Sea. However, L.15 was not so lucky.

It was first sighted over Orsett and several pilots – Second Lieutenant E.W. Powell of Sutton's Farm, Lieutenants Claude Ridley of Joyce Green, Kent and Alfred de B. Brandon of 39 Squadron at Hainault Farm, all located the airship. It was also heavily attacked by gun batteries along the Thames Estuary, especially those of No 3 Company of E.&S.R.G.A. at Purfleet where shells were seen to burst directly under the airship. Brandon dropped some explosive darts and bombs onto it. As L.15 was severely damaged, Breithaupt jettisoned his bombs and ballast near Rainham. He circled over Foulness before finally coming down in the sea near the Kentish Knock lightship about fifteen miles from Margate; Breithaupt and most of his crew were rescued by an armed trawler. The Lord Mayor of London awarded his prize of £500 to No 3 Company at Purfleet and Lieutenant Brandon; the money was used to strike suitably engraved gold medals. *The Times* reported:

Just as gunfire is a protective measure, so are aeroplanes when boldly and skilfully handled; and it is a combination of the two methods together with the development of searchlights, which will some day make it far more difficult for Zeppelins to raid our shores.

This optimistic view was a little premature because over the next four months there were another eight Zeppelin raids, several on consecutive nights. Precious few sightings were made by R.F.C. pilots, although on 24th/25th August L.31 was chased by Second Lieutenant Mackay of 39 Squadron based at North Weald Bassett but to no avail; he was running short of fuel and had to make an emergency landing at Burnham-on-Crouch landing ground. However, within a month or so four airmen from Essex landing grounds would strike a serious and crippling blow at the German Airship Service.

September 1916 proved to be a remarkable and successful month for the R.F.C. and more particularly for 39 Squadron. On the night of the 2nd/3rd the enemy launched a major bombing operation of fourteen Zeppelins and two Schutte-Lanz airships against London, Lincolnshire and Nottingham. During 'Zepp Sunday' (as it was called) over one hundred and sixty bombs were dropped and four civilians killed, but more famously Lieutenant W. Leefe Robinson of 39 Squadron at Sutton's Farm brought down S.L.11 in flames over Cuffley, Hertfordshire.

The blazing airship was seen for miles, even as far south as London, and many thousands claimed to have witnessed its final destruction. Leefe Robinson became a hero overnight; within days

The remains of Zeppelin L.32 at Great Burstead, Billericay – September 1916. (Illustrated London News)

SL.11 over Cuffley, Hertfordshire – September 1916.

he was awarded the Victoria Cross as well as receiving over £4,200 in prize money (a fortune in those days) as the first pilot to destroy an airship over the United Kingdom. Later Leefe Robinson was given the command of 48 Squadron which was then serving in France. In March 1917 he was shot down and taken prisoner. Perhaps weakened by his ordeal as a prisoner of war, Leefe Robinson died of influenza on 31st January 1919 aged thirty-three years; there is a memorial to him at Cuffley.

LIEUT. WILLIAM LEEFE ROBINSON, V.C.,
Worcester Regiment and R.F.C.,
Who brought down the Zeppelin at Cuffley, near Enfield.
ST. JAMES' PRESS, ROSOMAN ST., CLERKENWELL, E.C.

On the night of 23rd/24th September two Zeppelins were brought down by pilots of 39 Squadron. Second Lieutenant W. Sowrey of Sutton's Farm destroyed L.32, which came down in flames at Great Burstead near Billericay, killing all the crew. Many people in Essex saw the demise of this Zeppelin. The Rev. Clark at Great Leighs wrote: 'the light from the burning Zepp was so bright that you could have seen to pick up a needle from the road...It was a lovely sight to see it'!

Another Zeppelin, L.33, crash-landed near Little Wigborough after suffering severe damage from gun batteries and the attacks made by Lieutenant Brandon of Hainault Farm. *Kapitän* Böcker attempted to set fire to his Zeppelin before he and his crew were marched off to Peldon after surrendering to PC Charles Smith of the Essex Police, who became known as 'Zepp' Smith from then on! Both R.F.C. pilots were awarded the Distinguished Service Order.

As with the Cuffley airship, thousands flocked to the two sites to view the remains of the 'invincible Zeppelins', and special trains were even arranged from Liverpool Street station to Billericay in order to cope with the crowds of Londoners who wished to see what was left of L.32 at Great Burstead.

The reputation of 39 Squadron was even further enhanced when on the night of 1st/2nd October Lieutenant Wulstan Tempest of Sutton's Farm shot down L.31 near Potters Bar. Its Commander was the legendary *Kapitän-Leutnant* Heinrich Mathy, the veteran commander of the German Naval Airship Service. He and his crew were killed and his death had a profound effect on the Service; as a most experienced and determined leader Mathy was irreplaceable. Tempest, who had on this occasion taken off from North Weald Bassett, was also awarded the Distinguished Service Order.

After this night no airship managed to get through to bomb London again. Two more airships were destroyed in late November – one over Hartlepool and the other close to Lowestoft. It was now safe to say that the battle against the Zeppelins was virtually over and the German High Command was forced to devise another strategy if it was to bring Great Britain to its knees by a bombing offensive.

As a precursor of things to come a solitary L.V.G. biplane flew brazenly over London at noon on 27th November and calmly dropped six bombs near Victoria Station. The enemy biplane escaped unharmed although it later crashed near Boulogne. *The Aeroplane* magazine clearly viewed this incident as a prelude: 'when the aeroplane raids start and prove more damaging than the airship raids, the authorities cannot say that they have not had fair warning of what to expect'. Noel Pemberton Billing, now an Independent Member of Parliament, warned:

In the next summer we shall experience raids of a much more serious character than the Zeppelin raids. Aeroplanes may come over this country…at night and at 15,000 or 20,000 feet, they may drop their bombs and get back before we know where we are…

A rather percipient judgement that sadly proved to be accurate.

The country was unaware that the German High Command was assembling a fleet of large heavy bombers for a bombing offensive on London and the South East. The project was coded *Turkenkreuz* or Turk's Cross and the Force was named *Englandgeschwader* (England Squadron) under the command of *Kapitän-Leutnant* Ernst Brandenburg.

The heavy bombers – G.IVs and later G.Vs – were known as Gothas from the *Gothaer Faggonfabrik AG* that had first designed them in 1915. They were twin-engine biplanes with a wingspan of over 77 ft and more than 40 ft long, manned by a crew of three and armed with two machine guns. They cruised at 70 m.p.h., could operate from about 21,000 ft and carried a bomb load of between 600 and 1,110 pounds. They flew in tight formations to provide added fire-power and were really the forerunners of the heavy bomber formations of World War Two. By May 1917 *Kagohl* 3 comprising four *Staffeln* (Flights) was ready and in place at four airfields near Ghent in Belgium, merely awaiting orders from their High Command to bomb London.

About five o'clock on the afternoon of 25th May 1917 the first 21 Gothas crossed the Essex coast between the Crouch and the Blackwater bound for London. Several witnesses at Burnham-on-Crouch and Southminster described them as 'high white machines making a loud noise', 'they were of a silver colour and appeared like an aeroplane but with a noise like a Zeppelin', and 'they were flying very high, just specks in the sky'.

A solitary gun of a mobile battery at Burnham-on-Crouch fired shots at the formation and twenty aeroplanes from the Essex Flight Stations were sent up to intercept them. Captains C.B. Cooke and Claude Ridley of 37 Squadron from Rochford and Stow Maries respectively later complained that their B.E.12s were 'completely unsuitable for chasing such hostile aircraft...it took thirty minutes to reach 15,000 feet and by that time the enemy aircraft were thirty-five miles away...and our aeroplanes had no reserve of power at that height'.

German G.IV Gotha – 'the mobile magazines of death'. (Imperial War Museum)

They were two of the remaining seventy-one pilots to combat these 'Leviathans of the skies'; due to large losses of airmen on the Western Front and in the absence of airships the number of Home Defence airmen had been almost halved. On this occasion London was saved by heavy cloud and the operation was aborted. But on their flight back to Belgium, Folkestone was heavily bombed, which caused widespread damage and killed 95 people with another 200 injured.

Eleven days later (5th June) twenty Gothas appeared above the Thames Estuary. Some bombs were dropped on Shoeburyness and Great Wakering but London was again saved by the weather conditions. Brandenburg decided to divert to a secondary target – the port of Sheerness on the Isle of Sheppey. Although over forty

R.F.C. airmen were in action, only one Gotha was brought down – by anti-aircraft fire. The *Daily Telegraph* was not unique in praising the Home Defence: '[it] was so effective that they only succeeded in penetrating the coastal districts for a few miles'. A far more realistic appraisal would have been that it was clear that it was to be only a matter of time and favourable weather before the Gothas reached London.

On 13th June the Gothas struck London a fearful blow, which proved to be the heaviest air-raid of the war; it caused considerable damage, killing 170 people and injuring another 430. The worst disaster was caused by the bombs that fell on a school at Poplar, where eighteen children were killed and many more injured. The day, which became known as 'Black Wednesday', caused a national outcry. *The Times* wrote: 'it slew women and children as well as men…and increased the utter and most universal detestation with which the Hun is held by the people of this country'.

'Black Wednesday' also led indirectly to the formation of the Royal Air Force. Faced with public and press outrage, David Lloyd George, the Prime Minister, selected the South African General Jan Smuts to head a committee to examine the defensive arrangements of the Home Defence and 'the existing aerial organisation for the study and higher direction of aerial operations'.

Despite all the brave attempts of the airmen from Essex and Kent landing grounds, it was quite clear that their aircraft were woefully inadequate for the task and that there were no accepted tactics for attacking a formation of strongly armed bombers. However, there was some consolation for the H.D. pilots on 16th June when Zeppelin L.48 was brought down by the combined efforts of Lieutenants Robert Saundby and F. Douglas Holder and Sergeant Sidney Ashby of the Experimental Station at Orfordness, along with Second Lieutenant Loudon P. Watkins of 37 Squadron at Goldhanger. L.48 crashed in flames near Theberton in Suffolk and on board was *Korvette Kapitän* Victor Schutze, the Commander of the North Sea Airship Service. It was the fifth and last Zeppelin to be brought down on British soil.

The three pilots were awarded the Military Cross and Sergeant Ashby received the Military Medal. Watkins was killed in action over France in July 1918 and Sergeant Ashby died in a flying accident in the same year, whereas Saundby reached the rank of Air Marshal. Douglas Holder, who had attended Felsted School, settled in Chelmsford after the war and became very involved in the civic life of the town – as J.P., Deputy Mayor and Alderman and Deputy Lieutenant of Essex. He died at Danbury in 1978 aged 81.

The Gothas returned on 4th July and, although extensive damage was sustained at Harwich and Felixstowe, the casualties were relatively light – forty-seven, of which seventeen were fatal. Three days later London was bombed and the damage was estimated at over £¼ million with fifty-seven fatalities. One Gotha was shot down in the Thames Estuary by R.F.C. airmen of 50 Squadron and

Air-raid damage in Southend-on-Sea, 1917.

another two were brought down over the North Sea by R.N.A.S. pilots.

The most severe raid on an Essex town came on 12th August when 34 bombs were dropped on Leigh-on-Sea, Shoeburyness and, mainly, Southend-on-Sea. 33 people were killed and 46 injured, some of them day-trippers waiting for a train at Victoria Road station. As the Rev. Clark recorded: 'many of those that suffered were from Braintree – munitions workers – there for the Bank Holiday week when the works were closed'. Although on this occasion over 130 sorties were flown by H.D. pilots, only one Gotha was shot down, having been chased all the way to the Belgian coast by a R.N.A.S. pilot from Walmer in Kent. However, another twelve Gothas were lost when close to their airfields due to engine failures and shortage of fuel.

This was the last daylight air-raid; from now on the Gothas operated by night and they were joined by the massive *Zeppelin-Staaken Riessenflugzeug* heavy bombers known as 'Giants' or 'R-planes'. They had a wing span of 140 ft, were powered by four engines and could carry up to 2,200 pounds of bombs. During the last week of September Gothas and Giants attacked London and 69 people were killed.

These night raids brought additional problems for the Home Defence pilots because, unlike the large Zeppelins, they were difficult to locate in the night skies. It was not until 18th December that the first Gotha was destroyed at night by a H.D. fighter flown by Captain G. Murliss-Green, the Commander of 44 Squadron, in his Sopwith Camel. He first attacked one over Essex but the Gotha eluded him. He returned to Hainault Farm to refuel and finally engaged another Gotha over Kent; this one did not escape, crashing into the sea off Folkestone. Two pilots of 44 Squadron – Captain George Hawkwill and Second Lieutenant C. Brooks – destroyed a Gotha on the night of 28th January 1918. It crashed in flames near Wickford and was the first Gotha to be brought down on British soil.

Night flying was a most hazardous business and several pilots from Essex landing grounds had narrow escapes whilst making emergency landings. During February 1918 two Goldhanger pilots, Second Lieutenants S. Armstrong and F. A. Crowley were killed as a result of landing accidents. Another tragic fatal accident occurred on the night of 7th/8th March when Captain A.B. Kynoch of 37 Squadron took off from Stow Maries in his B.E.12 at almost the same time that Captain H.C. Stroud of 61 Squadron left Rochford in his S.E.5a. The two aeroplanes collided in cloud over Rawreth and they fell in adjacent fields at Dollymans Farm, Shotgate, where there are two memorials to mark the sites of the crashes. On 29th July there was another mid-air collision at Fairlop, which caused the deaths of three airmen.

Later, in September, Captain L.G. Davies, a flying instructor at Fairlop, was killed in his Avro 504K whilst performing aerobatics

Officers of No 44 Squadron at Hainault Farm in 1918. (via G. Weir)

at Fairlop. He was the last airman to be killed during the war whilst flying from an Essex landing ground; but before Fairlop closed in 1919 another two airmen would be killed in flying accidents.

As a result of the recommendations of the Committee headed by General Smuts, the Air Force (Constitution) Act received the Royal assent in late November 1917. Thus the Air Ministry was formed in early January 1918, and with effect from 1st April 1918 the R.F.C and R.N.A.S. were formally amalgamated to be known as the Royal Air Force.

The night of 19th/20th May saw the last raid on London. Thirty-eight Gothas and three Giants bombed London, parts of Essex and Kent and they were opposed by eighty-four R.A.F. fighters. Six Gothas were destroyed by the Home Defence units, three by anti-aircraft fire

The memorials to Captains H.C. Stroud (on the left) and A.B. Kynoch in adjacent fields at Shotgate.

and the others by R.A.F. airmen. Captain D.V. Armstrong of 78 Squadron at Sutton's Farm engaged a Gotha over Orsett and he is believed to have seriously damaged it before his ammunition was exhausted.

It is not known whether this was the same Gotha that Lieutenant A.J. Arkell and his observer, First Airman A.T.C. Stagg. of 39 Squadron at North Weald Bassett shot down over East Ham in their Bristol fighter. This was the last enemy aeroplane to be destroyed by airmen flying from an Essex landing ground, although another Gotha with engine failure force-landed near Clacton and three crashed near their landing grounds in Belgium. Arkell, who entered the Church after the war, lived in retirement at Little Baddow near Chelmsford, where he died in 1980 aged 81.

Thus the 'blitz' on London, Essex and Kent had finally ended –1,414 people had been killed and some 3,410 injured between 1915 and 1918. These figures, tragic though they were, may be viewed as infinitesimal when compared with the *daily* casualty losses on the Western Front. Nevertheless, for the first time the full horrors of war had been visited upon the civilian population and the harrowing experiences were remembered by the public for many years to come. The 'blitz' had also ensured that aeroplanes and flying had lost their innocence and 'mystique' of the peacetime years and the Zeppelins, Gothas and Giants had clearly demonstrated to the public at large the darker side of aviation when they rained death from the skies.

Chapter 8

Peaceful Skies & Joy Riding (1919–1926)

On Monday, 11th November 1918, as the Great War came to a merciful end, the Royal Air Force was the largest air force in the world with well over 22,000 aircraft, some 100 airships, almost 3,000 officers and men and more than 400 landing grounds in the country. At the beginning of the war, aviation had been in its infancy and considered a novel and exciting sport enjoyed by a relative few – then there had been just 881 certificated pilots and over half were military airmen. A mere four years later the aeroplane had been developed into a potent fighting machine, and there had been innumerable advancements in design, performance, endurance and, moreover, safety.

The appearance of an aircraft in the skies had almost become a commonplace occurrence, certainly in Essex with its large number of landing grounds. Over 350,000 people nationwide had been involved in some aspect of aviation during the war, most in aircraft construction and many in the support services on the ground, besides all the pilots and observers actually engaged in flying. Thus a large percentage of a new generation had been introduced to the fascinating and thrilling world of flight.

Sir Sefton Branckner, a Member of the Air Council, wrote in the *Daily Mail*:

> The War has bequeathed to us as a nation, a great heritage of the air. Our pilots are the best, our designs the most efficient and our industry the greatest in the world. Supremacy in the air is ours for the making.

The county of Essex had played no small part in the development of this 'great heritage of the air'. In just ten years Lea Marshes, Barking and Fairlop had witnessed the early and faltering attempts of A.V. Roe and Frederick Handley Page, besides the other less successful experimenters at Dagenham, South Fambridge and numerous other places in the county. During the Great War so many brave airmen left the landing grounds in Essex in an attempt to counter the threat from the air.

As 1919 dawned no peace agreement had yet been signed so the R.A.F. remained virtually intact, at least until the treaty was finally signed on 28th June. Twenty landing grounds in Essex were still in the hands of the Air Ministry, although during the year as squadrons were quickly disbanded their landing grounds were handed back to their original owners. In February Shenfield, Chingford and Fairlop landing grounds closed and in the following month Goldhanger, Stow Maries and North Benfleet were vacated. During the summer Burnham-on-Crouch, Blackheath Common, Broomfield Court, Little Clacton and Wormingford closed down and at the end of the year the aircraft flying from Hainault Farm and North Weald Bassett suddenly left as the airmen were demobbed. The last two, Sutton's Farm and Rochford, were relinquished early in 1920. Most of the buildings were used for other purposes and later disappeared but the gravestones in several churchyards still bear testimony to the inherent dangers of flying and two village signs – Goldhanger and Stow Maries – proudly proclaim their wartime flying heritage.

The wartime restriction on civil and private flying was lifted on 1st May 1919 and the Air Navigation Regulations were introduced under the control of the new department of Civil Aviation, which had been established on 13th February. A British Civil Register was introduced, which required all civil aircraft to carry identification markings; originally starting from 'K100' onwards but in July changed to commence with 'G–EAAA'. Each aircraft was required to have a Certificate of Airworthiness and all 'commercial' pilots were required to pass flying tests in order to obtain a 'B' licence.

One of the first companies to enter into the field of passenger and freight air-transport was Handley Page Transport Ltd of Cricklewood. With typical foresight and entrepreneurial flair, Handley Page was well aware of the boundless potential of this aspect of air travel. He bought back from the Ministry of Munitions four new 0/400 heavy bombers at below the price he had sold them for and his company proceeded to convert them into passenger-carrying aircraft; they were the first civil aircraft to be registered under the new system.

On 1st May Lieutenant Colonel W.F. Sholto-Douglas, M.C., D.F.C., Handley Page's Chief Pilot and famous WWI airman, flew with eleven passengers from Cricklewood to Manchester – the first post-war passenger flight in the country. Ten days later Sholto-Douglas flew the same aircraft to Southend-on-Sea. He circled the pier before dropping a package containing the latest editions of the *London Evening News* by parachute. The parcel was recovered by a motor-boat and was formally delivered to the Mayor, Alderman F.W. Senior, and other members of the Town Council, who had

A village sign proudly proclaims its wartime flying heritage.

gathered on the sea front to witness this historic event. This rather dramatic delivery of newspapers constituted the first recorded civil aircraft movement in Essex since the end of the war.

An Essex company was also quick to appreciate the potential of air travel. The Marconi Wireless Telegraph Company of Chelmsford aimed to be in the vanguard of airborne wireless telegraphy. During the war it had achieved a modicum of success in locating and tracking enemy airships and the company had now set up an Aircraft Department under H.C. van de Velde. It had purchased a de Havilland D.H.6 and began to operate it from the wartime landing ground at nearby Writtle. A wooden hut was erected to house the test equipment and the ground engineers. In the summer of 1919 van de Velde was the 'radio operator' on Handley Page's first experimental flight to Paris in a converted 0/400. He managed to make telephonic contact with Writtle and Cricklewood,

Handley Page, G–EAAF Vulture, *similar to G–EAAE that flew over Southend-on-Sea in May 1919.*

where a ground station under private licence had been established by the Marconi Company.

In early 1922 the company replaced its D.H.6 with an Avro 548 (G–EBAJ), which could regularly be seen in the skies over Writtle and Chelmsford at least until the summer of 1924. One local resident well remembered this aircraft some fifty years later; he described it as 'a bit like a frantic wasp buzzing around in circles all the summer long'! The 548 had first flown in late 1919 and it went on sale in March 1920 as the 'Avro Tourist'. It was a three-seat biplane (two passengers in tandem in the rear cockpit) with a Renault 80 h.p engine, and had a cruising speed of 65 m.p.h with an operational range of 175 miles. Marconi's 548 was equipped with an AD1/2 wireless set, which had a fairly reliable range of more than 100 miles.

Marconi Company's Avro 548 – G–EBAJ – was a familiar sight in the skies above Writtle and Chelmsford between 1922 and 1924.

The landing ground at Writtle was vacated in the summer of 1924 when Marconi's Aircraft Department moved to Croydon in Surrey. The Air Ministry had asked the company to establish a radio ground station at the new airport, then known as the London Terminal Aerodrome. The Wireless Operator at Croydon, F.S. Mockford, who was directly employed by the Air Ministry, is credited with introducing the 'talk-down procedure' for aircraft landing in poor weather conditions and also the international distress call 'Mayday' from the French *m'aidez* ('help me'). Mockford later became Commercial Manager of the Marconi Wireless Transmission Company.

Over the next few years the resurgence of civil and private flying in Essex was a little more mundane. Although there was a glut of ex-military aircraft available to purchase at bargain prices, the costs of maintaining a private aircraft had risen alarmingly, largely as a result of the new Air Regulations. Nevertheless there were a sufficient number of ex-Service pilots keen to try to take advantage of the public's increased interest in aviation, which had been fostered by all the exciting and heroic tales of the famous wartime pilots. They felt that this could be achieved by offering people the chance to experience 'the miracle of flight' for the first time by 'pleasure flights' or 'joy-rides'. Thus it was that 'joy-riding' became an essential feature of flying in the years ahead and such flights did so much to make the public more 'air-minded' and flying more popular.

In theory, joy-riding should have been a profitable enterprise but in the early 1920s it proved otherwise. The country suffered a severe economic recession with mounting unemployment. In these early days the normal charge for pleasure flights was a guinea (£1.05), then a small fortune and beyond the reach of most people, which was the main reason why so many small joy-riding companies failed to survive for more than a year or so.

Most of these companies used Avro 504Ks; between 1919 and 1930 over three hundred were allocated civil registrations and the 504K became the most ubiquitous aircraft to be seen in the country's skies and more especially at seaside resorts. It had first appeared in 1913 and was destined to become one of the most famous aircraft of all time with some 8,000 built until early 1927 when production ceased. The Model Js and Ks were the classic

One of the many joy-riding companies that operated in the 1920s.

Navarro Co. Ltd was one of the first joy-riding companies to operate in Essex.

training aircraft of the Great War; one distinguished pilot, H.R.H. Prince Albert (later King George VI) learned to fly in a 504J at Croydon.

Avro 504Ks were cheap to buy and there was a boundless supply of spare parts. It had a proven good safety record and many ex-Service pilots had been trained on them. Furthermore there was a ready pool of mechanics well experienced with its 100 h.p. Gnôme Monosoupage or 110 h.p. le Rhône engines; the latter gave it a top speed of 95 m.p.h but the 504K cruised comfortably at 75 m.p.h. Although it was never considered easy to fly, when mastered it was claimed to be a 'real pilot's aeroplane'. Over the next ten years or so many thousands of passengers would gain their first experience of flying in a 504K and forever afterwards fondly remember the experience.

The first joy-riding company to operate in Essex was the Navarro Company Ltd, originally based at Burton-on-Trent but later moving to Kingston-upon-Thames. The company had been formed by Joseph G. Navarro and in June 1919 he purchased three 504Ks, which he converted into three-seaters. Navarro employed several ex-R.A.F. pilots and during the summer began to offer joy-rides from Southend-on-Sea. Two of his 504s, flown by J. Thompson and R. Nicholson, operated from the wartime landing ground at Rochford.

Another company, the Central Aircraft Company of Kilburn in London, brought a Centaur IVB seaplane (another three-seater) down to Southend-on-Sea and, during the summer, the company's chief pilot, Herbert Sykes, offered pleasure trips over the town. It is believed that Alderman Senior was Sykes' first passenger; he was obviously very 'air-minded' and perhaps he thought he would set a good example to his fellow townspeople. None of these aircraft returned for the 1920 summer season. The Central Company concentrated on aircraft manufacture and its flying school at Northolt, whereas in May of that year Navarro had been forced to sell his 504s due to financial difficulties.

During the summer of 1922 Surrey Flying Services, based at Croydon, brought one of its 504Ks to Southend-on-Sea and Clacton-on-Sea to offer joy-rides to holidaymakers. The company had been formed in February 1921 by F. Grant and Captain A.F. Muir for joy-riding, air taxiing and flying instruction. It had introduced cheap 'round the aerodrome' trips at Croydon for five shillings (25p), which proved to be very popular. The company became one of the most successful in the field and survived well into the 1930s. It had also built three Avro 548s under contract, which included the one operated by the Marconi Company.

The first Essex airman to enter into joy-riding was Frank T. Neale of Thornwood, Epping. He formed Essex Aviation in January 1923 with a solitary 504K (G–EBCK), which he flew himself. Originally operating from a variety of fields in the north of the county, he then extended his area to Southend-on-Sea and later across the Thames to Margate and Cliftonville.

Another airman operating from Essex fields during 1923 – W.G. Pudney – was shown in the British Register as 'of Canvey Island'.

Pudney had originally bought his first 504K (G–EAMI) in September 1919 but it crashed near Banbury in Oxfordshire when he was a partner in Pudney-Brettel-Owen Ltd, based in the Midlands. Whether Pudney was born in Essex is not known; in November 1922 he purchased another 504K (G–EAJZ) and during 1923 he was offering pleasure flights at Canvey Island, Wickford and Orsett. His first recorded site was at Gidea Park on 28th January. However, in July he sold his aircraft and there is no record that he bought another 504K; he disappeared from the flying scene, at least as far as Essex was concerned.

Almost two years later the same happened to Neale; by early 1925 he had sold his 504K and there are no further references to him flying in Essex. Both men were the victims of the dire economic climate in the country and joy-riding did not return to Essex until the late 1920s.

Other than these rather brief forays into joy-riding, aviation in Essex appeared to be virtually moribund. During the early 1920s there were two small private licensed aerodromes in the county but whether there was much flying activity at either is rather uncertain. In 1923 it was reported that 36 acres of farmland on the east of Chingford's wartime landing ground was registered as an aerodrome known as Hall Lane. The other was at Fairlop, 25 acres directly to the west of the wartime landing ground, and was known as Forest Farm. Both aerodromes were regularly inspected by the Metropolitan Police as was required under the Air Regulations. In 1923 Forest Farm's licence was not renewed, but Hall Lane continued to operate until the autumn of 1934.

Chapter 9

The Return of the Royal Air Force (1927–1929)

The haste and urgency to dismantle the Royal Air Force during the immediate post-war years, when squadrons had been disbanded with an unseemly regularity, had backfired on the Government. In 1922 deep concern was expressed about the paucity of the Home Defence Force; at one stage there was just a solitary fighter squadron based in the country. The Government announced that the R.A.F. would be enlarged to nine squadrons; in June 1923 the new Prime Minister, Stanley Baldwin, increased the figure to seventeen, all to be operational 'within five years', although by the end of the decade there were only thirteen regular fighter squadrons. Nevertheless, the planned expansion programme dictated that new fighter aerodromes were needed to house these squadrons.

During late 1922 teams from the Air Ministry proceeded to seek out suitable sites within a 20-mile radius of London. In Essex a team viewed possible areas of land at Romford, Grays, Ockendon, Ingatestone and Orsett but came to the conclusion that the WWI landing grounds at Sutton's Farm and North Weald Bassett were the most favourable for development. In fact the latter had not been relinquished by the Air Ministry but rather placed under 'Care and Maintenance', though in truth very little 'care and maintenance' had taken place there. In July 1923 a compulsory purchase order was sought for 120 acres at Sutton's Farm, where the farmer, Tom Crawford, was back farming. The owners of the land, New College, Oxford, agreed to the sale and work on the new aerodrome started in May 1924. Building work at North Weald Bassett did not commence until early 1926.

The construction of permanent R.A.F. stations during the inter-war years was completed to a remarkably high standard with the provision of fine brick buildings, permanent tarmac roads, the inevitable parade ground, normally three large hangars incorporating workshops, a watch office (later known as a control tower), barrack blocks for the airmen, dining rooms and cookhouse, a sergeants' mess, airmen's married quarters, ample sporting facilities, an imposing entrance and a guard room. Invariably the Station Commander's house, the officers' mess and the officers' married quarters were situated outside the close confines of the station, as was the case in both of the Essex airfields.

These 'Expansion' stations, as they were known, provided a standard of elegance and comfort quite unique for the time and their outward appearance helped to foster the belief that the Royal Air Force was 'the best flying club in the world'. Many of these buildings at North Weald survive 80 years later. As to the airfield proper, all permanent stations were provided with grass runways; concrete runways were only belatedly introduced in the late 1930s and then only at a handful of bomber airfields, with one notable exception.

The new station at North Weald Bassett formally opened on 27th September 1927 but it was known as R.A.F. North Weald. The first Station Commander was Wing Commander A.G. Garrod,

Siskin IIIAs of No 56 Squadron arrived at R.A.F. North Weald in October 1927.

M.C., D.F.C., but its first fighter squadron, No 56, did not arrive until 11th October.

The squadron had been formed in November 1916 and had achieved considerable success and fame during WWI when it was credited with the destruction of 395 enemy aeroplanes and six balloons. Amongst its pilots were two holders of the Victoria Cross – Captain Albert Ball and Major McCudden. It had reformed at Hawkinge in November 1922 after serving in Egypt. The squadron was destined to remain at North Weald until June 1941, except for occasional breaks, and its Hurricane pilots fought with fine distinction during the Battle of Britain. It was now commanded by Squadron Leader C.H. Elliott-Smith, A.F.C., and amongst its young pilots was Flying Officer T.G. Pike, who later became a Marshal of the Royal Air Force.

No 56 Squadron was equipped with the Armstrong Whitworth Siskin IIIA, which had first flown in May 1923 and had entered service in March 1924. It was the first biplane to be provided with 'vee' interplane struts and also the first of an all-metal construction. The Mark 'A' was powered by a supercharged 460 h.p. Jaguar IVS engine giving it a top speed of 156 m.p.h at sea level but 142 m.p.h. at 15,000 ft. It had entered service in September 1926 and equipped eleven squadrons until it was replaced in October 1932. The Siskin proved to be an exceptional fighter for its time and was a superb aircraft for aerobatics, as their memorable displays at Hendon and other air shows fully testified. Indeed, in March 1928 No 56 Squadron took part in a demonstration of 'air manoeuvres' at Hendon on the occasion of a state visit by the King of Afghanistan. The feature of the display was that the pilots were controlled by R.T. (radio telephone) from the ground.

The second squadron, No 29, arrived at North Weald in April 1928 and was also supplied with Siskin IIIAs. The squadron's origins could be traced back to November 1915 and, after being disbanded, it had reformed at Duxford in April 1923 as part of the Expansion plan. It would remain at North Weald for the next nine years.

After nearly four years of construction Sutton's Farm was ready for occupation in the spring of 1928 and it was formally opened on 1st April. Squadron Leader Keith Park, M.C., D.F.C., brought his squadron, No 111, from Duxford to occupy the new station. The squadron had been formed in Palestine in August 1917 and had reformed in October 1923, originally with Gloster Grebes but now its pilots were also flying Siskin IIIAs. Thus these pugnacious biplanes became very familiar sights in the Essex skies as their pilots practised their various flying routines, formations and aerobatic displays, which formed so much a part of the life of fighter squadrons during the late 1920s and early 1930s.

In June the new station's name was changed to R.A.F. Hornchurch and Squadron Leader Park became its first Station Commander. Park, a New Zealander, gained lasting fame as an Air Vice-Marshal when he commanded No 11 Group of Fighter Command with great distinction during the Battle of Britain. One of No 111 Squadron's young pilots was Pilot Officer Frank

The entrance to R.A.F. Hornchurch in 1928. (R.A.F. Museum)

Whittle, who gained immortal fame as the designer of the jet engine. The squadron remained at Hornchurch until 1934 and three years later it became the first squadron to receive the R.A.F.'s first monoplane fighter – the legendary Hawker Hurricane. Both stations were placed under the control of 'The Fighting Area' of the recently formed Air Defence of Great Britain (A.D.G.B.).

In the late 1920s as the economic state of the country gradually improved there was a fresh impetus given to private and civil flying. The exploits of the various long-distance pilots, both civil and Service, had created immense public interest and inspired countless young people to join the swelling band of private pilots. Alan Cobham had become the most celebrated airman of the day, closely followed by Bert Hinkler, but the number of female pilots, such as Lady Mary Bailey and Lady Heath ('the flying aristocrats'), making the headlines proved that flying was certainly not the sole preserve of the male world. Lady Mary du Carroy, the Duchess of Bedford, who had taken her first flying lesson at the age of 62, also clearly demonstrated that flying was not just for the young. The 'Flying Duchess', as the press fondly called her, was hardly ever out of the newspapers. Aero or flying clubs were springing up throughout the country; many of them were financially sponsored by the Air Ministry. Also the appearance, in February 1925, of a quite

Squadron Leader Keith Park, M.C., D.F.C., became the first Station Commander of R.A.F. Hornchurch. (R.A.F. Museum)

remarkable aircraft – de Havilland's D.H.60 Moth – had a dramatic effect on private and club flying and really stole the thunder of the Avro 504Ks.

Nevertheless flying remained largely the preserve of the rich and relatively well-off members of society. A new Moth cost £650 and a course of flying lessons to obtain an 'A' licence could amount to £75 or more. Despite the resurgence of private flying there was not, as yet, an Aero or Flying club in Essex, the nearest was Suffolk Aero Club at Hadleigh, which had been formed in 1925. For the majority of people the only way to get a taste of flying was by taking a joy-ride – either a 'five-bob flip' (25p) or a longer flight for fifteen shillings (75p). A number of joy-riding companies regularly plied their trade, particularly at Canvey Island, Southend-on-Sea and

Lady Mary du Carroy, the 'Flying Duchess', in May 1927 with Captain C.D. Barnard. (via R.M. Roberts)

Clacton-on-Sea during the summer season, but some other companies also used inland fields around the county.

Surrey Flying Services had returned to Southend-on-Sea and vied for customers with the red Avro 504s of the Cornwall Aviation Company, which had also been in the joy-riding business since 1924. During the summers of 1927 and 1928 the Henderson School of Flying of Brooklands brought its Avro 548s – G–EBSC and G–EBWH – to Canvey Island and used a field next to Andrews Fair and close to the Casino. The latter 548 was damaged on landing at Canvey Island on 22nd July 1928 and was found to be beyond repair, although neither the pilot nor his passengers were injured. Colonel G.L.P. Henderson had set up his flying school in May 1926, the first post-war school at Brooklands, but by the end of 1928 he decided to retire from aviation.

In April 1928 a field at Maylands Farm, Harold Wood, was first used as a landing ground, the very modest beginnings of what in the 1930s became the most famous airfield in the county. A.H.

Surrey Flying Services returned to Southend-on-Sea during 1927/8.

Matthews, a flour miller from Battlesbridge, had purchased a 504K (G–EBSJ) and had arranged with G. Gothridge, the farmer, to lease a field at Maylands as a private landing ground. The sloping field was situated alongside and to the north of the main A12 road and was about three-and-three-quarter miles to the north-east of Romford. Matthews retained his aeroplane until July 1934 and continued to use Maylands aerodrome, although by then it had been greatly developed.

Later in April, Matthews was joined at Maylands by British Flying and Motor Services Ltd; its directors were H.P. Cochran, D.B. Hope and Mrs W.E. Coates, who was shown as 'The Chairman'. The company operated two D.H.6s (G–EBVS and G–EBPN) and an Avro 548 (G–EBPJ), which were engaged in joy-riding 'from fields throughout Essex'. The 548 crashed at Maylands on 31st July 1928 and its British registry was allowed to lapse. For whatever reason the company did not survive for very long because in March 1929 it sold its two aircraft to Arthur 'Art' Forsyth and Randall Ward, who formed Inland Flying Services on 6th April; they also owned an Avro 504K (G–AAET; in July the Civil Registration lettering changed to recommence from 'G–AAAA').

Avro 548 – G–EBSC – of the Henderson School of Flying at Canvey Island in the summer of 1928. (via H. Thomas)

After just one summer season of joy-riding around the county, the company moved to Shanklin on the Isle of Wight, where the name was changed to Wight Aviation Ltd.

In 1929 another Essex company made a brief foray into joy-riding – Aeroplane Services Ltd of Park Road, Leyton, E14; it was owned by Albert J. Adams and two brothers, C.C. and C.H. Bint. Adams and C.C. Bint were experienced in joy-riding having previously flown for the Cornwall Aviation Company, when Adams was billed as 'the daring aerial acrobat'. They operated a 504K (G–AAEZ) from 'The Flying Ground' at North Finchley. During the summer their 504 offered pleasure flights from a field at Shoeburyness in direct competition with Surrey Flying Services. Business could not have been very brisk because the company went into voluntary liquidation in December 1929. Adams returned to Cornwall Aviation but whether the Bint brothers remained in aviation is not known.

Sir Alan Cobham, as he was now, started his long and exhausting flying tour of the country in May 1929; it was his attempt to

Sir Alan Cobham's D.H.61 Giant Moth – G–AAEV – Youth of Britain.
(via Colin Cruddas)

persuade local authorities to establish their own aerodromes – the 'Municipal Aerodromes Scheme'. For this quite remarkable tour Sir Alan flew his D.H.61 Giant Moth named *Youth of Britain*. Besides giving flights to Mayors and other local dignitaries, Sir Alan had been sponsored by Lord Wakefield to offer free flights to schoolchildren. His tour lasted until October and he visited over 100 cities and towns and in the process carried over 100,000 schoolchildren as well as over 40,000 other passengers.

Cobham's arrival in a town created immense interest and excitement, although, due to his tight schedule, he only stayed for a day. Sir Alan arrived at Chelmsford from Dover on 14th August and his *Youth of Britain* used Baddow Meads alongside the Chelmer as a landing ground. In September he visited Colchester but neither borough financed a municipal aerodrome; the only one in Essex was established by Southend-on-Sea Corporation in the 1930s, which was one of the few towns of any size or consequence that Sir Alan Cobham did not visit!

During the late 1920s R.A.F. squadrons based in Britain had mainly 'a decorative role' to play; they gave air demonstrations for important foreign visitors and performed at the various and numerous air shows throughout the country and, of course, at the annual R.A.F. Display held at Hendon. Since the first R.A.F. Tournament (as it was then called), which had been held in July 1920, attendance had increased markedly and the Display had become an important feature of the summer aviation scene. Besides the remarkable and spectacular air displays, the public were also able to view the latest Service aircraft. On 27th June 1929 a record crowd of 170,000 attended the Display, evidence of how flying had captured the public's imagination and interest.

Perhaps because of its proximity to London and the convenience of a nearby railway station, R.A.F. Hornchurch was used by the Air Ministry as one of their 'show fighter stations' and it played host to a number of important visitors. On 28th June 1928 General Italo Balbo, the Commander of the *Regia Aeronautica* (Italian Air Force) led a formation of eleven aircraft on a non-stop flight from Rome to Hornchurch. The formation was met over the Essex coast by five Siskins of 111 Squadron to escort them into Hornchurch. Balbo was the proponent of the use of large aircraft formations and the term 'Balbo' was used in WWII to describe the use of two fighter wings. Just over twelve years later, on 11th November 1940, two Hurricane squadrons from North Weald wrought havoc amongst fifty bombers and fighters of the *Regia Aeronautica* attempting a daylight bombing raid on Harwich, when twelve Italian aircraft were shot down without loss.

In January 1928 a new Station Commander was appointed to North Weald – Wing Commander Sholto-Douglas – who had piloted the first civil flight over Southend-on-Sea back in May 1920.

His sojourn at North Weald was relatively brief; he left in August 1929. In November 1940 he became A.O.C. of Fighter Command and he retired from the Service in 1947 as Marshal of the Royal Air Force. In early April 1928, No 56 Squadron won the Sir Phillip Sassoon Map Reading Cup, a prestigious award for navigation, and later in the month Sir Phillip, the Secretary of State for Air, visited North Weald for an official inspection and to formally present the Cup.

The three Essex squadrons gave a splendid aerial display over Cranbrook Park, Ilford on 10th September 1929 on the occasion of the British Legion Carnival Fete. There had been mounting criticism of squadrons giving such displays but Lord Trenchard, Marshal of the Royal Air Force, remained adamant that they should continue to take part. He considered that as the general public was funding the R.A.F.'s expansion, it was 'only fitting and proper that their aircraft and pilots should appear at such shows, they helped to make the country more aware of the excellence of the Air Force and also more "air-minded".'

Thus, as the decade came to a close, it might be said that aviation in Essex was beginning to emerge from the doldrums. Military aircraft had returned to its skies and the first private aerodromes had opened. Over the next ten years flying in Essex would increase dramatically with one operator, Hillman's Airways, leading the way with the provision of cheap air travel. Exciting days were just around the corner.

Chapter 10

'Cometh The Hour, Cometh The Man' (1930–1932)

owards the end of the decade the prospects for aviation appeared promising but the 'Wall Street Crash' of October 1929 brought in its wake the most severe economic depression suffered by the country since the end of the Great War. Unemployment reached two million and continued to rise in the following years.

Nevertheless, despite this deepening recession private and club flying not only managed to survive but in fact it prospered. By 1931 it was estimated that over 2,000 persons held 'A' licences and another 300 possessed 'B' licences, which enabled them to carry passengers and fly commercially. *Country Life* magazine estimated that the annual cost of flying varied between £200 and £300 depending on the type of aircraft and mileage flown; this was without the initial purchase of a light aircraft – say £500–£600.

Edward Hillman at Maylands with his Puss Moth, Gilford.

One newspaper columnist recognised the wide disparity in society when he commented on 'those favoured few in their expensive flying machines peering down like gods upon those less fortunate beings patiently queuing for their dole money'.

Passenger air travel had also increased quite markedly but the high cost of a ticket ensured that it, too, remained the privilege of 'those favoured few'. However, there was one man, Edward Henry Hillman, who had plans to bring air travel within the reach of most people, and in the process he altered the aviation scene in Essex almost single-handed.

Despite the harsh economic climate, the public remained completely fascinated with flying, the numbers attending air displays (especially Hendon) steadily increased and the daring exploits of a number of pilots engaged on solo long-distance flights became front-page news, their progress avidly followed by the public. In this respect 1930 was a remarkable year. In January

Francis Chichester flew to Australia in his Gipsy Moth. Then, in April, the indomitable Duchess of Bedford arrived back at Croydon to great acclaim after completing a round trip to Cape Town in twenty days.

But the airwoman who captured all the headlines and the public's adulation was Amy Johnson – 'the little typist from Hull'. In May she completed her solo flight to Australia in her Gipsy Moth, *Jason*, to become the first airwoman to accomplish such a flight. 'Amy, Wonderful Amy' became an instant celebrity and was rarely out of the news during the 1930s; she would later be briefly involved with aviation in Essex.

The impression that women aviators, or 'petticoat pilots' as they were famously called by one celebrated male pilot (Charles Scott), were dominating long-distance flying was only reinforced when, on 25th September, an Essex-born lady, the Hon. Mrs Victor Bruce, set off at dawn from Heston in her Blackburn Bluebird IV on a solo flight around the world.

By any standards, let alone those of the time, she was a most incredible woman. Mildred Mary Petre was born on 10th November 1895 at Coptfold Hall, Margaretting near Chelmsford, the daughter of Laurence and Jennie Petre; yet another member of this old and famous Essex family to take to the skies. At the age of 16 she was the first young lady to be brought before a court for speeding – 67 m.p.h. – on her brother's motor-cycle! Four years later she bought her own motor-cycle and, after her marriage to the Hon. Victor Bruce (a well-known motor racing driver) in 1926, she successfully took part in several Monte Carlo rallies, raced at Brooklands motor track and along with her husband, drove in several 24-hour endurance trials. In 1929 she turned her attention to motor-boats and immediately proceeded to set several speed records.

In June 1930 she saw a Blackburn Bluebird IV on display in a shop window (Auto-Auctions Ltd) in Burlington Gardens, London and immediately realised that she now wanted to learn to fly, but furthermore with the avowed ambition of 'flying round the world in it'! Within days she had bought the aircraft at a cost of £560 and arranged for an additional 50-gallon fuel tank to be installed in the place of the second seat.

There was now just the little matter of learning to fly. Like all her other sporting activities, she accomplished this with apparent ease at the Blackburn Aeroplane Company's flying school at Brough in Yorkshire. Just eight weeks after receiving her 'A' licence and with only forty hours of solo flying to her name, she set off on what she described as 'my long flight or odyssey'.

Her all-metal biplane, G–ABDS, which she had christened *Bluebird*, had a Gipsy II 120 h.p engine which gave a maximum speed of about 110 m.p.h. and cruised at 85 m.p.h. The Bluebird IV had first appeared in February 1929 and came onto the market in the following summer; 58 were ultimately produced and they found favour with flying schools, aero clubs and racing enthusiasts.

Mildred's planned route was east to Munich, Istanbul, Hong Kong and on to Tokyo; from whence she travelled by steamer to

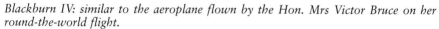

Blackburn IV: similar to the aeroplane flown by the Hon. Mrs Victor Bruce on her round-the-world flight.

Vancouver. From there she flew down to Los Angeles before crossing America to land at Boston and on to New York. Another sea voyage was taken to Le Havre before making the relatively short flight to Croydon. On the morning of 20th February 1931 Mildred landed at Croydon having been escorted from the English coast by Amy Johnson and Winifred Spooner (another celebrated woman pilot). She was formally welcomed home by Mr Montague, the Under-Secretary for Air, on behalf of the Air Ministry. Her journey of some 20,000 miles by air and sea was described as 'of epic proportions under most extreme conditions'.

She had joined the ranks of celebrated women pilots, who were now sufficiently numerous to warrant their own Challenge Cup donated by Lord Northesk and, in the summer, over 40 of them attended the first all-women's flying meeting at Sywell aerodrome in Northamptonshire. In 1932 Mildred Bruce founded Luxury Air Tours Ltd and also conducted air-to-air refuelling experiments, which though unsuccessful pre-empted those of Sir Alan Cobham two years later. In 1977 her autobiography, *Nine Lives Plus: Record Breaking on Land, Sea and in the Air,* was published. This grand lady died in May 1990 at the age of 94, after a long and most extraordinary life.

During 1930 most of the flying activity in Essex was undertaken by the fighter squadrons based at North Weald and Hornchurch. In

Bristol Bulldogs of No 54 Squadron at Hornchurch.

'The petticoat pilots' at Sywell aerodrome, September 1931. Third from the left is Pauline Gower, then the Hon. Mrs Victor Bruce and at the end, right, the Duchess of Bedford.

January a new squadron, No 54, arrived at Hornchurch with its Siskin IIIs and it remained there for the next eleven years, most notably during the Battle of Britain. In April the Siskins were exchanged for Bristol Bulldog IIAs. This fighter had first flown back in May 1927 and it would epitomise the R.A.F. during the coming years. The Bulldog was a fast aircraft for those times – top speed 178 m.p.h – and moreover it had fine aerobatic qualities. They were particularly noted for their highly polished cowlings and squadrons took an immense pride in maintaining their machines in pristine and immaculate condition. Hornchurch's other squadron, No 111, received its Bulldogs in early 1931, followed a little later by 56 Squadron at North Weald. It had been a difficult and tragic year for North Weald. The Station Commander, Wing Commander

The Hon. Mrs Victor Bruce on her return from her round-the-world flight.

Smythes, D.F.C., was killed in a D.H. Moth and on 4th November Flying Officer R. Bennet of 56 Squadron was killed in his Siskin when it crashed near Ingatestone.

Towards the end of the year a flying club was formed that was open to aspiring pilots living in Essex although the Herts & Essex Flying Club found a home at a new small aerodrome at Broxbourne, in Hertfordshire, not far from the county boundary. The aerodrome received its licence in November but it was not formally opened until the following June. The first flying club based in Essex was formed in 1931 – Southend Flying Club, at Canute Air Park at Ashingdon, some four miles north of Southend-on-Sea.

Another small Essex aerodrome opened in Essex during the year. It was at Blue Barns Farm, a couple of miles north-east of Colchester and just to the east of the A12 road. It was planned to operate as the Essex branch of the Eastern Counties Aeroplane Club, which had recently been formed at the new aerodrome at Ipswich in Suffolk. The club had two Robinson Redwing II biplanes, one of which, G–ABNP, was based at Blue Barns Farm.

During the summer of 1931 the first touring air displays, or 'flying circuses' as they were invariably billed, made their appearances at several locations in the county. The North British Company Ltd was the first to arrive; it was based at Hooten Park, Liverpool and had been formed by Lance J. Rimmer, a well-known airman. The company started its 'Tour of Britain' in April with several Avro 504Ks and its display offered 'aerobatics, crazy flying, formation flying, balloon bursting and parachute descents' along with passenger flights 'from 3/6d'; the cost of admission was 6d for adults with children half-price. On 29th July its air display was held at Nash Farm, Clacton-on-Sea, on 9th August at 'The Aerodrome, Clacton' and later in the same month (26th) at Dovercourt. On 13th September they were at a field at 'Crabb's Farm, Hamstel Road, Southchurch', which must have proved successful because the display returned to the same site on another two days – the 20th and 27th – which in fact ended their 1931 tour. The company remained in the profitable business of air displays until 1935 but it did not return to any Essex fields again.

For virtually the next six years the British summer scene was not complete without such air displays. Most of the various companies involved were led by celebrated aviation personalities, perhaps the most famous of whom was Sir Alan Cobham.

Despite the appearance of these flying circuses, without doubt the highlight of the aviation season in 1931 was the first flight of de Havilland's D.H.82 Tiger Moth, which took place on 26th October. The Tiger Moth was destined to become one of the most (if not *the* most) famous training aircraft in the world. In February 1932 it was adopted as the standard R.A.F. trainer *ab initio* and was not completely replaced in the Service until 1955. The Tiger Moth was quickly accepted by flying training schools and private owners and

D.H.82 Tiger Moth arrived on the aviation scene in October 1931.

over 8,800 were finally produced. Despite the economic depression de Havilland's was one of the few aircraft manufacturers not only able to survive but to actually prosper during such uncertain financial times.

As far as Essex was concerned the outstanding feature of 1931 was the arrival, in November, of Edward Henry Hillman onto the flying scene. Over the next three years he would become the most enterprising and influential man in Essex aviation.

Hillman had been born in Croydon in 1889 into a family of humble circumstances. At the age of twelve he joined the Essex Regiment as a drummer boy and by the end of the Great War he had attained the rank of Sergeant-Major in the cavalry. Hillman now entered the world of motoring as a Rolls-Royce chauffeur for the Diplomatic Service. His innate entrepreneurial skills led him to set up a small shop at Stratford for the hire, sale and repair of bicycles. He later bought a motor-car to begin a car-hire and taxi service.

By early 1928 Hillman had acquired sufficient funds to purchase his first motor-coach, which he drove along with his 16-year-old

Robinson Redwing – three were built at Colchester. (via S.M. Brown)

son. By December he had established a regular service from Stratford to Brentwood, which was later extended to Chelmsford and Colchester. Over the next two years Edward Hillman's Saloon Coaches Ltd burgeoned to over 50 coaches and it had extended its services as far as Clacton-on-Sea. His success enabled him to purchase a substantial house in Hare Street (now known as Main Road), Romford and, no doubt rather proudly, his own Rolls-Royce motor-car!

Despite the dire economic plight of the country, Hillman, with considerable foresight, recognised that there were great possibilities in the future of air travel; originally air-taxi and charter work and then to expand into the world of passenger travel. He envisaged a cheap air service for 'those who rode in my buses'. With this thought in mind he purchased two de Havilland D.H.80A Puss Moths, which probably cost him in the region of £2,000. The Puss Moth had first flown in September 1929 and they were on sale in the following March. The aircraft cruised at about 108 m.p.h, the passenger and pilot sitting in tandem in the cabin, although a second passenger could be carried for short journeys. Hillman's Puss Moths, G–ABSB and G–ABSO, were named *Sonny* and *Babs* respectively, and another, G–ABVX *Gilford,* was bought later.

The next step was to acquire an aerodrome and, on 26th November 1931 Hillman's Saloon Coaches & Airways Ltd obtained the licence of Maylands aerodrome from A.H. Matthews. Hillman now set about developing the aerodrome with the erection of three large hangars, workshops, a control office, a passenger reception area, booking office and a restaurant. Harald Penrose, the celebrated test pilot and later famous aviation writer, who met Hillman on a number of occasions, described him as 'a colourful tough, rough and forceful character, who was determined to have "no 'igh fallutin pilots, I got young 'Timber' Woods wot was a sergeant pilot and 'ee and two others does the flying".' Henry W. 'Timber' Woods, Hillman's Airways' Chief Pilot until 1935, had served in the R.F.C/R.A.F. as a Flight Sergeant and during the 1920s had toured the country demonstrating the new Irvine parachute to R.A.F. personnel.

Hillman's Airways were soon offering 'Aerial Trips Daily from 8 a.m. till Dusk and Passenger Trips at 5/-, 10/- and £1…First-class Comfort, First-class Pilots, First-class Planes from Maylands Aerodrome'. Long-distance charter flights were based on 3d per mile and it is interesting to note that in May 1931 *Country Life* magazine had estimated the cost of private air travel at about $^3/_4$d a mile, and that in those days the cost of petrol was in the region of 1s 4d a gallon (about 6p)! But Hillman had far more ambitious plans for his small airline.

It is open to debate whether Hillman's enterprise and early success had any influence or bearing on the sudden development of aviation elsewhere in the county. Certainly from 1932 until the outbreak of war in September 1939, the amount of flying – commercial, club and private – increased dramatically, as indeed did Service flying. However, this escalation might more realistically reflect the general trend that was taking place throughout the country, when the next few years or so would, in hindsight, be recognised as 'The Golden Age of Flying'.

In January 1932 Aviation Transport Sales & Services Ltd had acquired the lease of the wartime landing ground at Broomfield, near

Sir Alan Cobham's National Aviation Day toured Essex during 1932.
(via Colin Cruddas)

Chelmsford, which Chelmsford & District Flying Club had been using for several months. Captain Heinz Talbot-Lehmann was the leading light behind the project and on 18th May the Lord Lieutenant of Essex, Brigadier-General R.B. Colvin, formally opened the aerodrome. The official ceremony was also commemorated by a visit from Sir Alan Cobham's Flying Circus. On 25th May the aerodrome received a Royal visitor when H.R.H. Prince George, Duke of Kent, arrived in his own aeroplane. He had several official duties to undertake in Chelmsford – visiting the Marconi Telegraph Company and Hoffman Manufacturing Company as well as Crompton Parkinson, although his main duty was to formally open Princes Way, the town's new A12 by-pass route.

Captain Talbot-Lehmann had plans to establish his own flying circus and by June, his two pilots – L.G. Ramsey and John Rogers – along with a parachutist and 'wing-walker', were giving air displays in the locality in an Avro 504K and two Klemm L.25 monoplanes. These were quite popular German light aeroplanes that had first appeared in this country during 1929. It is believed that Talbot-Lehmann was also of German origin. On 18th September there was a rather disastrous fire, which destroyed and damaged some of the aeroplanes, and the aerodrome never really recovered. Certainly no touring air displays used it again; in fact, in July 1933 when the British Hospitals Air Pageant visited Chelmsford, it used a field at Springfield, not that far from Broomfield aerodrome.

In direct contrast, Blue Barns Farm aerodrome near Colchester actually became busier during 1932. In February, Redwing Aircraft Ltd (formerly Robinson Aircraft Company Ltd) moved its manufacturing base from Croydon to Colchester and ultimately three Redwing IIs – G–ABRM, G–ABRL and G–ABNX – were built there. The first Redwing had appeared in May 1930. It had been designed by Captain Phillip G. Robinson, and he claimed it was 'a gentleman's aeroplane with no vices and [it] would be extremely safe to fly'.

Hillman's Airways' D.H.83 Fox Moth – G–ABVI.

HILLMAN'S
SALOON COACHES
AND AIRWAYS

HEAD OFFICE - LONDON RD., ROMFORD
Phone Romford 1705 (2 lines.)
Clacton Office - HILLMAN'S KIOSK, 125 OLD ROAD
Phone Clacton 62.
Aerodrome - ALTON PARK, CLACTON-ON-SEA
Phone Clacton 62.

AERIAL FLIGHTS
——DAILY——

9 a.m. TILL DUSK   Popular Trips at 5/-, 10/-, £1
First-class Comfort, First-class Pilots, First-class Planes

A Plane at Clacton Aerodrome.

The Clacton Aerodrome is situated from Warwick Castle
Hotel down St. Osyth Road, then first turning on left.

Poster for Hillman's Airways Service to Clacton Aerodrome. (via M. Robinson)

Although only twelve Redwings were built, it was described by the aviation press as 'a superb light aircraft...with good lines...docile handling qualities...and provided with folding wings for easy storage'. Although priced most competitively at £575, the aircraft lost out to the Tiger Moths that were now flooding onto the market.

On 10th March the Aero Club celebrated the resurgence of Blue Barns aerodrome by holding a 'winter meeting' when a new clubhouse was formally opened by Charles W.A. Scott, the celebrated pilot. Redwing Aircraft Ltd was not destined to stay at Blue Barns for very long. In May the company purchased Gatwick aerodrome in West Sussex, which had opened two years earlier and was then known as Lowfield Heath. The following July the company gave notice of the sale of the aerodrome and by late February 1934 Redwing had moved back to Croydon. Thus the very brief and only instance of aircraft manufacture in Essex since the end of the Great War came to an end.

Despite this, there was a report that 'Mr R.N. White of Grays, Essex built a small Canard aeroplane in 1930/1', and also that two Avro 504Ks were being reconstructed from spare parts 'in a garage at Orsett for Essex Flying Club at Abridge'. This small aerodrome was also known as Loughton and is thought to have opened in the summer but it was not officially registered until 29th November. The two Avros were finally completed and one, G–ABWK, did in fact go to Abridge. The other one, G–ABYB, was sold to Captain Talbot-Lehmann at Chelmsford but it was struck off the British Register in June 1933, which further suggests that Broomfield aerodrome had a very brief existence.

The first of Edward Hillman's ambitious plans was realised on 1st April 1932 when his small Airways Company commenced a scheduled service to Alton Park aerodrome on the outskirts of Clacton-on-Sea with his three Puss Moths and a recently acquired D.H.60G Moth. The journey time was about 30 minutes compared with some 3–4 hours by one of his coaches, and a single fare cost 12s 6d whereas a return could be obtained for £1. This constituted the first air passenger service from an Essex aerodrome.

Sir Alan Cobham's boundless enthusiasm for aviation had led him to establish a touring air show, which was formally registered as 'National Aviation Day [later Display] Ltd' but would soon be far better known as 'Cobham's Flying Circus'. He had assembled a small fleet of aircraft including two Airspeed Ferries, several Moths, a number of Avro 504Ks, a Cierva C.19 Autogiro, a BAC Glider and a Desoutter monoplane. He also employed a number of pilots, wing-walkers and parachutists. Sir Alan aimed to bring the thrills of flying to hundreds of cities and towns throughout the country and provide the public with a highly expert and exciting air show.

The first tour commenced in mid-April and arrived in Essex on 17th May at Maylands; the following day it had moved to Broomfield aerodrome to coincide with the official opening. The next day it operated from Blue Barns Farm aerodrome and one week later (26th) it gave a display at Goodmayes Park, Ilford. On 26th July 'the Flying Ground, Alton Park Road, Plough Corner, Clacton' was its next venue in Essex; then, on 16th October, Hall Lane aerodrome Chingford was visited as the last of 175 different sites throughout the country that had been used. Over the next three years Cobham's Flying Circus visited a number of aerodromes and landing fields in Essex. Although a number of other air shows and pageants would tour the country until 1937, by common agreement there was no doubt that Sir Alan Cobham's display led the field.

In January de Havilland's produced yet another winner in their Moth series of aircraft, the D.H. Fox Moth. As *Flight* magazine commented: 'carrying a pilot and, for short distances, four passengers on a single Gipsy III engine of 120 h.p. must be regarded as very economical flying indeed'. The aircraft cruised at about 105 m.p.h and had a range of just over 400 miles. It seemed an ideal aeroplane for Hillman to use on his Clacton service, especially as economy was always his abiding watchword; indeed it was rumoured that he paid his pilots only slightly more than his bus drivers! In next to no time Hillman had bought two Fox Moths, G–ABVI *Chris* and G–ABVK *Doreen,* to add to his growing fleet.

Possibly Hillman had been so impressed by Sir Alan Cobham's very professional air display at Maylands back in May, that he planned to stage his own special air show there. It was advertised as 'The Greatest Civil Air Display of the Year' with a 'gathering of Britain's most famous pilots, including Mr and Mrs J.A. Mollinson [Miss Amy Johnson]'. It was held on Saturday, 24th September and he had obtained the patronage of the Lord Lieutenant of Essex and the Lord Mayor of London, Sir Maurice Jenks. He and his Lady Mayoress, along with other London civic dignitaries, arrived at Maylands from Heston aerodrome in a Spartan Cruiser, which was the first time a Lord Mayor had travelled by air to an official event.

The day proved to be a spectacular success, even Bulldogs from 54 Squadron gave a display and there was a special air race from Maylands to Clacton for the Hillman Trophy, which was won by Hugh Buckingham, an employee of de Havilland's, flying rather appropriately a Fox Moth. Over 2,000 spectators attended and passenger flights were given until dusk. The air show ended with a 'Grand Firework Display'. It was abundantly clear that Edward Hillman was quickly making his mark in the world of aviation.

Spurred on by the success of his Clacton service, Hillman had plans to extend his services to Paris. He had been most impressed by the performance of his Fox Moths but considered that he needed a larger passenger aircraft to make such a service profitable. Hillman was quite undaunted by Geoffrey de Havilland's reputation as a designer and he visited him at Hatfield with the suggestion that his company should consider developing a larger and twin-engine version of the Fox Moth. According to Sir Geoffrey's autobiography *Sky Fever*:

One day Edward Hillman came to discuss the possibility of a small airliner. Hillman was a remarkable man. He had been running a bus service of his own, even driving the vehicles himself when he first started. With unbounded energy he had built up a sound organization and now had greater ambitions to start a

London–Paris air service … His enthusiasm was contagious, and we at once looked into an eight-seater airliner, using two Gipsy Major engines and Tiger Moth extension wings. The fuselage, tail unit, landing gear, controls etc. were, of course, new. *The success of the Dragon design was largely due to Hillman's far-sighted and courageous action in ordering a small fleet of them 'off the drawing board'.* [My italics]

Thus were born de Havilland's most remarkable, elegant and classic series of Dragon small airliners that became the mainstay of the country's growing number of civil airways during the 1930s and even into the post-war years.

In fact de Havilland's design team had already been working on a project for the Iraqi Air Force, which they regarded as a 'double Fox Moth'. As mentioned above, after viewing the drawings Hillman immediately ordered four Dragons before the first aircraft had been even built, let alone trialled. Ultimately the prototype D.H.84 Dragon made its maiden flight to Maylands aerodrome on 12th December, flown by Hubert Broad, the company's Chief Test Pilot. It was flown back to Hatfield for further tests before being delivered to Hillman's Airways just eight days later.

Hillman had managed to persuade Mrs Amy Mollinson to officially christen the new aircraft, although she had only just returned from one of her many long-distance flights, this time from Cape Town. Thus on 20th December G–ACAN was appropriately named *Maylands*. Subsequently Hillman's Airways operated another five D.H.84 Dragons – G–ACAO, G–ACAP, G–ACBW, G–ACEU and G–ACEV – which were named *Goodmayes, Brentwood, Romford, Gidea Park* and *Ilford*. Edward Hillman was now on the threshold of his cherished ambition of providing cheap air travel, and furthermore he was quite prepared to take on the might of the prestigious Imperial Airways on its Paris service. All this had been achieved in barely twelve months since he had obtained the lease of Maylands aerodrome.

Chapter 11

The Golden Age of Flying (1933–1935)

After the horrors of the Second World War many people would look back in fond nostalgia to these 'golden days of flying'. During those somewhat fleeting summers hundreds of thousands flocked to the various air displays and pageants that were held up and down the country. The numerous 'flying circuses' that toured the country vied with each other to bring more spectacular and thrilling aerial exploits to attract an eager public and they brought back the sheer joy and excitement of flying.

New and innovative aircraft regularly appeared and several would become 'classic aircraft' still highly revered even today. Private and club flying prospered with many more people taking to the skies for the first time. Largely through the endeavours of Edward Hillman there were far greater opportunities for affordable

Sir Alan Cobham's 'Flying Circus' comes to town. (via Colin Cruddas)

air travel within the country and to the near Continent. The Royal Air Force opened its gates for the first time; these 'open days' were relaxed and informal affairs and they gave the general public the chance to view 'their Air Force' and its aircraft at close quarters. The economic state of the country had slowly improved and, as yet, the public were not aware of the dark clouds that were gathering over Germany, which in a few years would darken such blue, tranquil and peaceful skies.

In January 1933 Edward Hillman, along with members of the Ramsgate Council, flew from Maylands to Manston aerodrome in

Kent in his new Dragon, G–ACAN, which was resplendent in the Airways' livery – half blue and white. The reason for this flight was to discuss Hillman's planned service to Manston to carry holidaymakers to the resorts of Ramsgate, Margate and Broadstairs.

The twice-daily summer service started on 8th April, but just eight days earlier Hillman's bold ambition had finally been realised when his Airways flew its first scheduled service to Paris. Only a year or so before, Hillman had boasted to reporters, 'I am going to run to Paris like a bus service from my field at Maylands. You'll see!' He had managed to set his fares at the bare minimum – £3 10s. for a single, £5 10s. for a return and a special weekend return (Friday to Tuesday) for £4 10s. Not only were these fares considerably lower than those of Imperial Airways but the flight time was 30 minutes less. Two daily flights left Maylands at 10 a.m. and 1.45 p.m. and returned from Paris at the same scheduled times. In July the Airways extended its Paris service to Vichy, although only during summer weekends. Hillman's Airways was now a force to be reckoned within the fast- growing world of air passenger travel.

The aerodrome at Piggott's Farm, Abridge had been taken over by Commercial Airways (Essex) Ltd, which had registered as a company in March. They formally announced rather grandiose plans 'to work lines of aerial conveyance between Loughton and all other parts of the world'! The company also owned the flying club, now known as the East Anglian Aero Club, which was certainly active in May, operating an Avro 504K and three ex-R.A.F. Bristol fighters or 'Brisfits'. The clubhouse was formally opened in June and in the following month (23rd) over 4,000 people attended an air display given by the London General Omnibus Company Flying Club, which had been formed at Broxbourne aerodrome two years earlier, to provide heavily subsidised flying training to its employees.

Since the pioneer days motor-cars and aeroplanes had been closely linked, as many of the early motoring enthusiasts were also pioneer airmen. From 1930 the Automobile Association had offered its members an 'aviator's weather information service' from Heston and it also provided continental touring maps for those few intrepid members flying to the Continent. A.A. patrolmen were frequently in attendance at aerodromes and air shows to offer their members assistance. In 1933 the Association published its first 'Register of Approved Landing Grounds', which provided information on the landing surfaces, nearby obstructions, storage, the nearest hotel, garage and telephone.

The only 'landing ground' in Essex to appear in the Register was at Burnham-on-Crouch. It was to the west of the wartime landing ground and closer to the town. The aerodrome was owned by the Royal Corinthian Yacht Club, presumably for the use of club members because a 'landing fee' of five shillings was charged to visitors. On 27th August 1934 the Duchess of Bedford formally opened the small aerodrome. The Duchess, now in her 69th year, arrived in her Gipsy Moth, G–AXBR, accompanied by her 'Flight Manager', Flight Lieutenant Ralph Preston. She recorded in her diary that they had experienced 'a very boisterous flight to Burnham' from her home at Woburn Abbey, where she had her own landing ground. After the formal ceremonies had been completed, 'the Commodore, Mr Mitchell took me on a sail along the river, it was equally rough...'!

Southend Flying School had moved to a new site 'in the centre of the Rochford Pony Track alongside Ashingdon Road and was managed by Southend Flying Services. It operated a number of aircraft – D.H.60 Moth, Puss Moth, Blackburn Bluebird III, Simmonds three-seat Spartan and an Avro 638 Club Cadet. The Club Cadet was a small and neat biplane that had first flown in May 1933 and was an improved model of the earlier Cadet, which Avro hoped would compete favourably with de Havilland's Tiger Moth. Southend Flying Services bought the first Club Cadet, G–ACAY in June and over the next twelve months another five were purchased; as only seventeen were produced the Flying Club

Avro 638 Club Cadet – G–ACIL – of the Southend Flying Club was lost in November 1935. (via S.M. Brown)

had the largest fleet of Club Cadets in the country. All but one survived at Southend until 1940 when they were broken up; one, G–ACIL, crashed at Thundersley on 22nd November 1935 and was destroyed.

Perhaps somewhat encouraged by Hillman's Airways' summer service to Manston, Southend Flying Services started a daily service ('on the hour, every hour') to the recently opened Rochester aerodrome, which was now leased to the aircraft manufacturers, Short Brothers. From the summer of 1934 the cross-Thames service was shared with Short Brothers. The cost of a single flight was eight shillings and twelve shillings for a return flight that on average took a mere twelve minutes.

Shorts used one of their new Scion 1s, G–ACJ1, on the service, mainly to publicise their new small 'air liner'. It had first flown on 18th August 1933 and was a twin-engine high-wing monoplane that cruised at about 100 m.p.h. and carried five passengers. Eighteen Scions were built and they operated very successfully on short-distance flights. Two Scions completed over 1,000 flights on

The British Hospitals' Air Pageant toured in 1933.

the short route from Rochester and were flown by Shorts' test pilots, J. Lancaster Parker and Harold Piper. It was estimated that over 1,400 passengers had been carried and another 400 or so had taken joy-rides. The service continued well into the summer of 1936 when Southend Flying Services also operated a Scion, G–ADDN.

During the summer of 1933 Sir Alan Cobham's National Aviation Day again visited a number of locations in Essex. It had expanded and Sir Alan was able to mount two separate tours – No 1 Tour was at Central Park, Dagenham whereas No 2 began from 'Holt Farm, Ashingdon Road, Rochford', where it would return for a repeat performance on 22nd August. During May, No 1 Tour performed at Blue Barns aerodrome on the 14th, followed by Palmers Farm, Shenfield (the site of the wartime landing ground) on the 23rd,

Short Scions were flown on the Rochester to Southend service.

The Hon. Mrs Victor Bruce and her Miles Satyr.

before appearing at Alton Park, Clacton-on-Sea five days later, and towards the end of the month (29th) from Standford's Farm, Queenborough Lane, Braintree. No 2 Tour brought its summer season to a close on 8th October when a display was given at Maylands aerodrome.

The Tours had visited over 300 towns during which time thousands of passengers were taken up on their first flight. It is remarkable how many R.A.F. airmen in the Second World War recalled that their fascination of flying had been first kindled by attending one of these air shows.

For this summer only Sir Alan had a serious competitor – the British Hospitals' Air Pageant (B.H.A.P.) – which had been organised by Jimmy McEwan King and Harry Barker. One of the objects of the B.H.A.P. was to raise funds for local hospitals; it was agreed that the nearest hospital to any given locality would receive ten per cent of the day's takings and one-third of the programme sales. The two men had assembled three parachutists and fifteen celebrated pilots, each flying their own aircraft; they included Charles W. Scott (Chief Pilot), Captain Phillips of Cornwall Aviation, Pauline Gower, a well-known aviatrix and that intrepid lady – the Hon. Mrs Victor Bruce.

Mildred Bruce was one of the leading stars of the Pageant, not only with her Miles Satyr, G–ABVG, which she had specially bought for aerobatics, but for her speciality – the 'Fox Dive'. She had purchased an ex-R.A.F. Fairey Fox, G–ACAS, for a mere £12 and offered spectators 'the thrill of a lifetime in the Fox Dive'. She took her Fox and hapless passenger into a vertical dive, only pulling out about 50 feet from the ground and then flying low and fast over the crowds – all this excitement for 15 shillings!

B.H.A.P. visited eight locations in Essex: Ilford (14th/15th April), Chingford on the 23rd and then Blue Barns aerodrome on 14th May. During July the Pageant came to Central Park, Dagenham on the 23rd, Alton Park, Clacton a day later, Rochford on 23rd/24th and Springfield, Chelmsford the following day. Towards the end of its tour Abridge was visited on 1st October and a week later it finished its season at Woolwich.

With Hillman's Airways operating their services from Maylands and Southend Flying Services from Rochford, along with all the air displays throughout the county, there were more than ample opportunities not only for taking a flight for the first time but also to see a wide variety of aircraft and to witness the daring and thrilling exploits of many celebrated pilots; 'Golden days', indeed. However, *Flight* magazine did issue a note of caution about these 'flying circuses': 'there is a risk that these air displays will give many the impression that flying means risking one's life and that pilots are a race of supermen...'. Nevertheless, they attracted the crowds in their thousands and as Sir Alan Cobham stressed, 'they did make Great Britain more air-minded'.

On 8th November Hillman formed a new company, Edward Henry Hillman Ltd, in place of Hillman's Saloon Coaches and Airways. However, early in the new year he would suffer a severe blow when, in January 1934, the London Passenger Transport Board took over most of his coach routes and also many of his coaches, which now numbered over 130. He did receive £145,000 in compensation which helped to increase his fleet of airliners.

Hillman was aware that Maylands aerodrome was not large enough for his expansion plans and he was busy arranging the purchase of 180 acres of farmland at Stapleford Tawney near Abridge for his new aerodrome. He now discovered that he would have to move sooner than originally planned when he was informed that Maylands would only be licensed for 'a restricted size of aeroplane'. The development of the new aerodrome pressed ahead and, because it was a more isolated location than Maylands, he ordered the construction of twelve cottages along the Ongar Road to house his employees. The new aerodrome required three Boulton and Paul hangars, workshops, offices, a passenger terminal building with H.M. Customs accommodation and ample car parking.

Avro 642 – G–ACFV – of Midlands & Scottish Air Ferries used Maylands during April–June 1934.

Before Hillman's Airways left Maylands a new service to Liverpool, the Isle of Man and Belfast was opened in April, in partnership with Midland and Scottish Air Ferries. This brought another new small airliner to Maylands and it was *not* built by de Havillands. Midland and Scottish used their new Avro 642/2m, G–ACFV, perhaps better known as the Eighteen. It was a high-wing monoplane specially adapted to carry sixteen passengers and two crew members and was the only one of its kind built by Avro. It had been named the *Marchioness of Londonderry* but was not destined to remain on the service for very long because on 4th June it crashed in North Wales. The aircraft was recovered and subsequently rebuilt, quite remarkably ending up in New Guinea, where it was destroyed by the Japanese in 1942.

The first Empire Air Day was celebrated on Saturday, 24th May when 39 R.A.F. stations were opened to the public for the first time along with many civil and private aerodromes. The Empire Air Day was the inspiration of Air Commodore J.A. Chamier, the Secretary-General of the Air League of the British Empire since 1932. Chamier was quite determined to make the country and especially children more 'air-minded' – the 'buzz' words of the 1930s. The concept was successful from the outset; over 77,000 visited the R.A.F. stations and during the next five years the numbers would increase dramatically. Over 4,300 people visited Hornchurch and £180 was donated to the R.A.F. Benevolent Fund. The numbers were less at North Weald, with just over 3,000 people and takings of £127.

In 1934 there were two bomber squadrons for every fighter squadron but during the year another four fighter squadrons were formed, one at Hornchurch. On 12th July, 111 Squadron left for Northolt and was replaced by the reformed 65 Squadron under Squadron Leader R.O. Soden. This heralded the arrival of yet another fighter – the Hawker Demon. This two-seater biplane had first entered the R.A.F. in 1931 as the fighter version of the remarkable Hawker Hart light bomber. It was only slightly faster than a Bulldog but was armed with two Vickers guns and also a Lewis gun in the rear cockpit. At this time all air-gunners were Leading Aircraftsmen (L.A.C.); it was not until 1940 that the minimum rank for all categories of air crew became Sergeant.

During July, Hornchurch was honoured with a Royal visit. On the 13th H.R.H. Prince Edward, Prince of Wales arrived in his Dragon, G–ACGG, along with his personal pilot, Flight Lieutenant E.H. Fielden. The Prince, like his younger brother, was a qualified pilot and very enthusiastic about flying, invariably piloting his Dragon to official engagements. On this occasion he was en route to Dagenham to open Ford Motor Company's new and large factory.

In March 1934, Redwing Aircraft had finally moved from Blue Barns aerodrome and on the 12th of the following month the licence for Alton Park, Clacton was withdrawn, but it was no doubt still used by private owners. Broomfield aerodrome at Chelmsford had returned to farmland and in the autumn Hall Lane, Chingford finally closed. Although, set against these closures, Stapleford Tawney was ready for occupation in June, which Hillman rather

Hawker Demons arrived at Hornchurch with No 65 Squadron.

grandly called 'Essex Airport'! On the 3rd the Paris service was transferred to Essex Airport and Hillman had plans to modernise his fleet.

His favourite aircraft company had designed a new four-engine passenger aircraft which appeared in January – the D.H.86 Express. However, in truth he was more particularly interested in their design of an improved Dragon, which had first flown on 17th April. The D.H.89 Six, as it was originally known, was effectively a faster and more comfortable Dragon; its two 205 h.p. Gipsy Six engines (hence the name) gave it a cruising speed of 140 m.p.h., but perhaps what really attracted Hillman was the company's claim that it used only nineteen gallons of fuel per hour, making it a most economical airliner for six to eight passengers.

The Dragon Rapide, as it was called in February 1935, became the classic aircraft of the 1930s, with over 720 being built and richly deserving its title – 'The Queen of the Airways'. Rapides were still operating with small airlines until well into the 1950s and the military version, the Dominie, remained in service until 1955. Hillman immediately ordered three, G–ACPM, PN and PO, and became the first British airline to operate Rapides. Ultimately

One of Hillman's Airways' Dragon Rapides.

Hillman's operated eight; one, G–ADAH, has survived and is now on display in the Air and Space Hall of the Museum of Science and Industry at Manchester.

Essex Airport was soon in the news when it became known that Amy Mollinson had accepted a position as pilot with Hillman's. She had only recently returned from America and was keen to obtain a regular flying job. In 1933, on a previous visit to the States, she had briefly flown as a co-pilot with T.W.A. (Transcontinental & Western Airways). Her first flight from Stapleford Tawney was to Paris on 24th August and it was said that several passengers refused to fly with a female pilot! Amy's time at Hillman's proved to be very brief, as by mid-September she was compelled to relinquish her post in order to concentrate on the forthcoming MacRobertson Race to Australia, in which she and her husband, Jim, would fly one of the three de Havilland Comet Racers entered for this celebrated air race. Amy had every intention of returning to Hillman's after the completion of the race but circumstances dictated otherwise.

In October 1934 Hillman's Airways was again in the news but this time it was for tragic reasons. On the 2nd one of its Rapides, G–ACPM, came down in the sea about four miles off Folkestone,

Amy Mollinson (neé *Johnson*) *flew briefly as a pilot for Hillman's Airways.*

and the pilot, W.R. Bannister, and the six passengers were killed. The Official Inquiry into the fatal accident disclosed that the pilot did not have a navigator's licence, had not taken a course in blind flying and furthermore was inexperienced in radio communications. This ultimately led to far stricter regulations for the award of 'B' licences.

During the summer the National Aviation Day was still wending its way around the country, visiting 133 towns from mid-April to the end of September. The tour started on 14th April at Central Park, Dagenham and visited Ramsey near Harwich on 25th June and Blue Barns Farm the following day. On 28th August it performed at Holt Farm, Rochford, before moving to Frinton-on-Sea. The tour ended at Maylands aerodrome on 30th September, now far quieter than hitherto.

Two other air displays made brief appearances in the county. The Sky Devils Air Circus performed at Claybury, Woodford on 30th September and a very short-lived air show, the Flying Fair, appeared at Rochford from 31st March to 2nd April before moving to Maylands two days later. Although Aviation Developments Ltd, who operated the Flying Fair, had plans to visit 150 towns, the tour was abandoned in mid-April; at that time it appeared to have a single Redwing II, G–ABOK.

With the departure of Hillman's Airways, Maylands aerodrome reverted to purely club and private flying. It was occupied by Romford Flying Club, the Drone Flying Club and Essex Aero Ltd, which had been formed by Jack Cross, a former Chief Engineer of Hillman's Airways; he also became closely involved with the development of Ramsgate aerodrome. The British Aircraft Company's Drone was effectively a powered glider with a small 750 cc engine installed on the top of the wing. It had been designed, in November 1932, by Charles Lowe-Wylde, the country's leading glider pilot. The Drone cost only £275 and although it was rather slow and noisy, it was the first serious attempt to provide a safe and cheap introduction to flying.

The Postmaster General announced that Hillman's Airways had been awarded the contract of a daily postal service from London to Liverpool, Belfast and Glasgow. On 1st December Captain W. Anderson, D.S.O., Hillman's' Chief Pilot since 'Timber' Woods had left for General Aircraft, piloted Rapide, G–ACPN, on the first mail service northwards, and the inaugural southern flight was made by Captain C.E.W. Petty in another Rapide, G–ACEU. It was also announced that in future all first class mail to Europe would go by air rather than by sea, so the prospects looked decidedly bright for Hillman's European routes. Nineteen days later Edward Hillman decided to float his company on the Stock Exchange and within a few hours the five shilling shares were all taken up and thus Hillman Airways Ltd was born. The drummer boy had come a long way!

However, on 31st December 1934 tragedy struck the new company when Edward Hillman died. He was only forty-five years old. The sudden death of this self-made man and most colourful personality was a sad loss to commercial aviation. In just three years he had contributed in no small way to make air travel more accessible and popular – an earlier Freddie Laker. His family were forced to sell a large block of his personal shares and the control of the company passed to Erlangers, the merchant bankers, with Major J. Ronald McCrindle appointed Chairman. The change of ownership was one of the reasons why Amy Mollinson did not return to the Airways as a pilot.

Another calamity of a quite different nature struck the Airways in February 1935. As *The Aeroplane* reported:

A few minutes after D.H. Dragon, G–ACEV, of Hillman's Airways Ltd. left Essex Airport for Paris on February 12th, two young Franco-American women named du Bois [Jane and Elizabeth – 20 and 23 respectively] daughters of Mr Coert du Bois, United States Consul General in Italy, who were the only passengers as they had booked all the seats, threw themselves from the machine near Upminster and were killed. The pilot,

Mr J.P. Kirton, did not miss the passengers until some 45 minutes after leaving Essex Airport...He flew back to Essex Airport, where the lock of the door was found to be in order...Letters addressed to Mr and Mrs Coert du Bois, which were left in the machine, were read at the inquest and indicated suicide, and the jury returned a verdict to that effect.

It would appear that both of their fiancés had been killed in a R.A.F. flying boat accident.

The year was quite eventful for the R.A.F. It was, of course, the Silver Jubilee of their Majesties King George V and Queen Mary, and on 4th May 1935 both Hornchurch and North Weald marked the occasion with ceremonial parades. On 6th July, the R.A.F. was officially reviewed at Mildenhall by King George, the Prince of Wales and the Duke of York; most appropriately as the Service had originated during King George V's reign. Bulldogs of 54 and 56 Squadrons were amongst over 350 aircraft lined up for inspection; then in the afternoon the Royal Party adjourned to R.A.F. Duxford where they were treated to the 'largest fly-past in the world', in which both squadrons took part.

R.A.F. stations again opened for Empire Air Day and there was some slight increase in the numbers attending. The Service had begun to expand and it was announced that another seven fighter stations would be established over the next three years; one would be located in Essex – at Debden. However, with hindsight, perhaps the most auspicious day in 1935 for the R.A.F. (and the country) was 6th November, when Hawker's 'Fury Interceptor', K5083, made its first flight at Brooklands. In June the Air Ministry approved the name 'Hurricane' for the Service's first monoplane fighter.

Yet again, Cobham's 'Flying Circus' had set off in April on another grand tour of the country. Although there were two separate displays, Astra and Ferry Shows, they appeared at far fewer locations in Essex. On Sunday, 23rd June Maylands aerodrome hosted 'Sir Alan Cobham's Air Display', then on 8th July

Hawker's 'Fury Inceptor' – K5083 – made its first flight on 6th November 1935.

the Display was held at Maldon and the next day it moved to Walton-on-the-Naze. On 30th July, Ramsey near Harwich was visited. The Ferry Show performed at 'Burnt Mills Road, Nevendon, Pitsea' on 24th August, but little did those spectators realise that this would be the final appearance of Cobham's 'Flying Circus' in Essex, as they had become an essential part of the summer season. When the two tours finally ended in September, Sir Alan decided to sell his business as he considered that the best days of these aerial displays had now passed.

During 1935, despite the change of ownership, Hillman's Airways Ltd appeared to go from strength to strength. On 6th June a new service to Liverpool, Manchester and Hull was started and almost two weeks later another new European service commenced to Ostend, Brussels and Antwerp. The company had invested in three D.H.86s. These four-engine biplanes carried ten passengers in a quite luxurious cabin (at least according to the standards of the day) and Hillman's intended them for use on their Paris service. On 20th June their first D.H.86 Express, G–ADEA, was formally named *Drake* at Stapleford aerodrome by Lady Cunliffe-Lister, the wife of the Secretary of State for Air. This D.H.86, like the other two, G–ADEB and G–ADEC, carried the Airways' new livery – completely dark blue.

There had been aviation developments in the south of the county. Councillor G.E. Weber of Southend-on-Sea Town Council had been leading a campaign for the Corporation to purchase the site of a wartime landing ground at Rochford for development into a municipal aerodrome. The Councillor was utterly convinced of the potential of air travel; not only was he President of Southend Flying Club but also the Chairman of Southend Flying Services. In 1933 his persistence was rewarded and the Corporation bought the landing ground. Its preparation went ahead as did the erection of a hangar, grandstand and clubhouse in the south-west corner of the aerodrome.

Hillman's Airways' D.H.86 being named Drake *by Lady Cunliffe-Lister, 20th June 1935.* (via D. Brown)

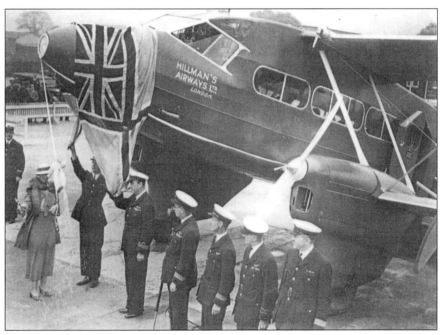

Early in 1935 the work was completed and Southend Flying Club moved in from their nearby aerodrome. In June the club members played host to 'young enthusiasts' of the local Skybird League. These clubs for young people interested in flying had largely been set up by the Air League of the British Empire. On 7th July, Crilly Airways began a Sunday service from Norwich which called at Ipswich, sometimes Clacton-on-Sea, and then Southend-on-Sea en route to Ramsgate; it operated until the end of September.

Councillor Weber was no doubt a proud man when on Wednesday, 18th September, Southend-on-Sea Municipal Airport was officially opened by Sir Philip Sassoon, the Under-Secretary of State for Air. He had arrived in his D.H.85 Leopard Moth. Many other celebrated figures of the aviation world also attended the grand opening, including Tommy Rose, the famous racing pilot. There was a fine gathering of aircraft and three of the Flying School's Club Cadets led the ceremonial fly-past. 'Special pleasure flights covering surrounding districts of Southend, Leigh and Westcliff' were also available either in an Avro 624 or de Havilland Dragon. It was an auspicious day for the County Borough as Southend (although invariably known as Rochford) was the only municipal airport in the county.

Also during September there were changes afoot for Hillman's Airways Ltd. It merged with United Airways and Spartan Air Lines and now came under the control of Whitehall Securities. A new company was registered on 30th September, Allied British Airways Ltd, but almost a month later the name was changed to British Airways Ltd. It was the largest private airline in the country and Major J. Ronald McCrindle was appointed its Managing Director. Several of Hillman's earlier Dragon airliners were sold before the end of the year and British Airways intended to move all its European services to Heston, so all the activity and bustle of Essex Airport would soon become a distant memory. Thus a brief but remarkable and most memorable period of aviation in Essex had drawn to a close.

Chapter 12

From Flying Fleas to Gladiators (1936–1937)

In early January 1936 Maylands' aerodrome licence was withdrawn, although it was still used for club and private flying until the outbreak of war; nevertheless its days of glory had gone by. There were plans to develop a golf course along the western boundary of the landing ground and the course was officially opened on 18th July; it is still flourishing 70 years later. British Airways had not quite vacated Stapleford, in fact on 17th February a new service to Malmö in Sweden commenced from there but did not run for very long. In May, British Airways was the first major airline to move all its services to the recently developed Gatwick Airport.

As an indication of the keen interest in affordable flying, Robert Kronfeld, the celebrated Austrian glider pilot, visited Southend

Flying Club on 23rd February to lecture on gliding. He had arrived at Rochford in his BAC Drone and later gave a flying demonstration. After the death of Charles Lowe-Wylde in May 1933, BAC (1935) Ltd had taken over the production of Drones at London Air Park, Hanworth, and Kronfeld was its Managing Director; also involved with the company was E. Gordon England, last noted with Pemberton Billing at South Fambridge.

It was claimed that the Drone was simple to fly and the cost of petrol for a trip to Paris amounted to only six shillings. Furthermore, taking into consideration all expenses (insurance, maintenance, depreciation and storage) the Drone cost a 'mere' 7s 6d per flying hour. Thirty-three Drones were ultimately produced and several flew in the British Empire Air Display of 1936. Later in the day Kronfeld gave a similar display to the members of the Aero 8 Club at nearby Canute Air Park. The club had been formed in 1935 by two engineers, Mervyn Chadwick and Raymond Gordon, especially for 'the development of the Flying Flea or Sky-Louse and/or other lower powered machines of a similar nature'; there was also a flourishing flying club which, at one time, had over 600 members.

Less than two months later (6th April) the Aero 8 Club hosted what was then called 'the greatest Flying Flea Rally ever'. The *Pou-du-Ciel* or Flying Flea was the brainchild of a Frenchman, Henri Mignet, who in 1933 had produced his H.M. 14 and had also committed to print his instructions on how to build a similar machine. When the Air League translated his book, *Le Sport de L'Air*, in 1934, the first edition of 6,000 copies sold out within a month. By the summer of 1935, it was estimated that may be 500 Flying Fleas were owned by enthusiastic amateurs. As one contemporary observer commented, 'the Flea craze is an astonishing revival of the spirit, which had earlier imbued the aviation pioneers'.

The original Flea was 12 ft long, 5 ft 6 ins high with a wingspan of 12 ft (when folded). It was said to be simple to construct with the minimum of hand tools and expertise, at a cost that varied from £50 to £100, and could be powered by a motor-cycle or small car engine. The members of the Aero 8 Club had developed their own variant, G–AEFW, which was powered by a Sprite 28 h.p. engine.

The Rally at Canute Air Park was a great success with Flying Fleas arriving from all over the country. However, several fatal accidents abroad cast serious doubts over its inherent safety, and the Air Ministry conducted a series of tests, which resulted in a refusal to grant any further Authorisations to Fly. Prior to this effective ban one hundred and nineteen had been placed on the British Register but no doubt hundreds more had been built or were under construction. On 17th May the Aero 8 Club's Flying Flea attempted a cross-Channel flight but it came down at Lympne. Nevertheless, many dedicated enthusiasts continued to work on creating a safe machine and the last fatal Flying Flea accident in Britain occurred on 29th September 1939.

'The Greatest Flying Flea Rally Ever' at Canute Air Park, 6th April 1936. (via D. Brown)

Two of the last 'flying circuses' toured the country and gave displays at several locations in Essex. The first to appear was the British Empire Air Display, which visited Abridge aerodrome on 28th June and was reported to have attracted over 5,000 spectators. The Display was organised by Jimmy McEwan King and Harry Barker but financed by the celebrated pilot, Tom Campbell Black, who with Charles Scott had won the MacRobertson Air Race in the previous October. Their senior pilot was Pauline Gower in her Spartan three-seater, flying alongside another eight pilots and three parachutists. There were several 504Ns, two Flying Fleas, a BAC Drone, Hawker Tomtit, Short Scion and a D.H.83 Puss Moth, G–ABVI, which had originally been owned by Hillman's Airways but was now registered by 'Hillman & Cross Ltd'; early in the tour it was damaged and withdrawn. The programme included formation flying, racing, aerobatic and stunt flying, wing-walking, parachute jumping and joy-riding (at Abridge alone Pauline Gower gave 51 joy-rides).

The following day the Display moved to Great Easton near Great Dunmow and on 1st July it was at Widford, near Chelmsford – the site of the old wartime landing ground – when over 2,000 attended and 38 joy-rides were given at five shillings a head.

The other company to tour during 1936 was C.W.A. Scott's Flying Display; it was jointly owned by Charles Scott and Captain

Supermarine 300 – K5054 – made its first flight on 5th March 1936.

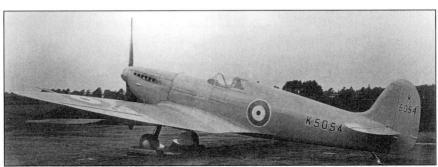

Percival Phillips who had purchased the goodwill and some of the assets of Cobham's National Aviation Displays Ltd; Don Eskell, Cobham's experienced General Manager, organised the tour. Scott was also the aviation editor of the *News Chronicle*. According to the posters, his air show was 'The "Flying for All" Display'. Eight well-known pilots were engaged, including Mrs Winifred Crossley who, along with Pauline Gower, became one of the first eight female pilots employed in the Air Transport Auxiliary in January 1940.

Besides the several aircraft that had operated with Cobham's Display, a couple of Drones and Flying Fleas were flown, as well as a Cierva Autogiro. The Display arrived at Rochford on 22nd July and just before the tour ended in late August, it performed at Pitsea. It seems that the tour was far from profitable, because on 23rd September the company was placed into receivership, a sign that attendances at such air displays had sadly fallen.

At Hornchurch there was a link with its wartime past when a new Station Commander, Wing Commander Arthur S.G. Lee, arrived; he had served at Sutton's Farm as a Lieutenant with 46 Squadron flying Sopwith Pups. In the summer there were major changes afoot

Gloster Gauntlet: the R.A.F.'s last open cockpit fighter.

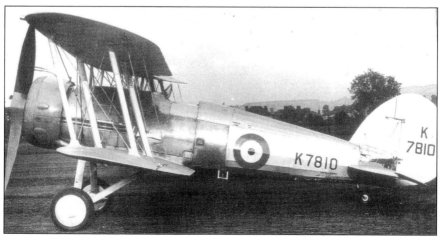

for the R.A.F. but perhaps the most momentous news of early 1936 was the first flight of Supermarine 300, K5054 at Eastleigh near Southampton on 5th March. Few people then appreciated the impact this aircraft would have. This new monoplane fighter, later to be named Spitfire, was so impressive that its test pilot, 'Mutt' Summers, told the design team 'don't touch anything'.

During the summer the Air Ministry placed large orders for these new fighters – 500 Hurricanes and 300 Spitfires – but nevertheless the next fighter to appear in Essex was still a biplane: the Gloster Gauntlet, which proved to be the last open cockpit fighter to serve in the R.A.F. It dated back to 1933 and had first entered service in May 1935. The two squadrons at Hornchurch, 54 and 64, changed to this new fast fighter (230 m.p.h.) followed by 56 Squadron at North Weald. When 151 Squadron was reformed at North Weald on 4th August it was also equipped with Gauntlets. By 1937 fourteen squadrons of Fighter Command were operating these biplanes, which gave the impression that nothing much had changed since the days of the Great War!

No 56 Squadron's badge.

Largely as a result of the planned expansion of the R.A.F. the Air Ministry reorganised the 'Air Defence of Great Britain' into four separate and functional Commands – Bomber, Coastal, Fighter and Training. Under the new system each Air Officer Commanding was responsible for the planning and development of their Command. Fighter Command was placed under Air Marshal Sir Hugh C.T. Dowding and comprised eighteen squadrons: fifteen regular and three of the Auxiliary Air Force. On 30th July another far-reaching innovation was announced – the formation of the R.A.F. Volunteer Reserve. Volunteers were recruited for a minimum of five years. They would receive flying training at weekends and during the mandatory annual fifteen-day summer camp.

In the previous year the Air Ministry had also agreed that all R.A.F. stations and squadrons would have their own special badge. To control their design and approval, an Inspector of Royal Air Force Badges was appointed – Sir John Heaton-Armstrong, M.V.O., who was then the Chester Herald at Arms. Each 'unit' or station was required to submit their design and motto for approval. These now familiar badges were surmounted by the Tudor Crown with the name or number of the squadron inscribed in gold lettering around the emblem, and a scroll bearing the motto. Most of the early badges were formally granted by King Edward VIII.

The mottoes of Hornchurch and North Weald were 'First Things First' and 'Offence Defence' respectively. No 56 Squadron's badge carried a phoenix to reflect its ability to reappear and the motto *Quid Si Coelum Ruat,* which translates as 'What if heaven falls'; whereas 65 Squadron's motto, *Vi et armis,* meant 'By Force of Arms'. The newly formed 151 Squadron carried on its badge an owl alighting on a seax (an ancient type of knife); the owl represented its night-fighting role and the seax from the Arms of Essex, which recognised its original formation at Hainault Farm in June 1918. It was the only R.A.F squadron badge to portray an affiliation with the county.

Despite the quite fundamental changes within the Service, life altered little for the squadrons based in Essex. It was all fairly leisurely and mainly comprised of practising for the various air displays and more especially Hendon, which this year was held on 26th June. The annual air exercises during the summer were the

C.W.A. Scott's Flying Display toured Essex in the summer of 1936.

highlight of the year. In July, for the first time the bomber attacking force came from the south-east, which provided the first major test for the Observer Corps on the ground; included in the 'targets' for the bomber force were Ford's car factory at Dagenham and the Marconi Works at Chelmsford.

Also in July (4th) three fighters from Hornchurch, a Demon, Bulldog and Gauntlet, made an unofficial visit to the Aero 8 Club at Canute Air Park and later gave a flying display or 'series of startling aerobatics', according to a local newspaper. Later in the month (21st) 56 Squadron's Bulldogs were sent to France, where five days later they had the honour of taking part in a fly-past at the unveiling of the splendid and dramatic Canadian War Memorial at Vimy Ridge.

In the summer Atlas Air Services made some improvements to Abridge aerodrome and in September Abridge Flying Club was formed. This small aerodrome would always suffer from being so close to Stapleford (three miles). On 1st September 1937 its licence was revoked and the aerodrome fell into disuse. Although no longer 'Essex Airport', Stapleford was still used for private flying, perhaps most notably in September when a prototype cabin monoplane, G–AENU, made its first flight from there. It had been designed by an Australian, Geoffrey Wickner, who had gone into partnership with Jack Foster and James Lusty, a furniture manufacturer. The aeroplane had been built in East London and was perhaps unique in being powered by a Ford V8 motor-car engine. Although the first flight was successful, the aeroplane failed to obtain a Certificate of Airworthiness. After some design changes and the substitution of an aero-engine, eleven Wickner Wickos were built and they sold for just under £1,000.

Further south at Canute Air Park, Chadwick and Gordon had plans to build a single-seat monoplane and on 2nd November 1936 they formed Premier Aircraft Constructions Ltd for this express purpose. During the winter of 1936/37 the aeroplane was built in a workshop at Harold Wood with the assistance of S.C. Buzzard, a

Three Gordon Doves were built at Harold Wood during 1936/7. (via B. Harrison)

young designer. The two engineers had been inspired by the Tipsy S, a small Belgian single-seater which had first appeared in this country in May 1936.

The prototype Gordon Dove, G–AETU, was taken to Maylands aerodrome on 3rd March 1937, where it successfully made its first flight under the control of Claude Oscroft, previously the Chief Pilot of the Aero 8 Club. By the end of the month the Dove was on display in a large London department store priced at £225, which included free flying tuition up to a Class 'A' licence. The Dove, later described as 'one of the most attractive light aircraft ever built', was powered by a 28 h.p. Sprite engine, which had earlier been used on the club's Flying Flea. The Dove had a top speed of maybe 95 m.p.h. and cruised at 85 m.p.h. There were plans to build another seven Doves but only two more were completed – G–AEZA and G–AEZB.

The Coronation of King George VI on 11th May 1937 was celebrated by ceremonial parades at Hornchurch and North Weald and it indirectly brought an added excitement to North Weald. In the early evening of 10th May two record-breaking American airmen, Richard Merill and John Lambie, arrived at North Weald in their Lockheed Electra, having completed a non-stop flight from New York. After the formalities were completed they flew on to

Gloster Gladiators arrived at Debden in June 1937. (R.A.F. Museum)

Croydon. Three days later they flew back to New York carrying photographs of the Coronation for the New York newspapers. Although the Atlantic had been flown by a number of airmen and airwomen, this was the first time the dual crossing had been made for purely commercial reasons.

At Maylands aerodrome the First National Aviation Club planned five days of aerial displays and pleasure trips to mark the Coronation but the bad weather prevented any of them taking place. Later in the month (27th) a Gloster Gauntlet of 65 Squadron at Hornchurch crashed on the corner of the airfield and its pilot, Sergeant Frederick W. Boxall, was killed.

The final 'flying circus' to tour the country was appropriately named the Coronation Air Display and was owned by those veterans of such displays – Harry Barker and Jimmy McEwan King. It must be admitted that it was a mere shadow compared with the air pageants that had previously toured the county. There were just three Avro 504s and a solitary parachutist. Although the Display toured 33 towns (mainly in Ireland), it only performed at one location in Essex – Galleywood Road, Great Baddow, Chelmsford on 24th April. The tour was a financial disaster and the reasons for this were said to be 'the omnibus strike, poor weather and a decline in public interest in air shows'! Yet on Empire Air Day held on 28th May over 350,000 people visited fifty-three R.A.F. stations; over 17,000 attended at Hornchurch and the day was blessed with glorious sunshine.

During the year there was a greatly increased R.A.F. presence in the county. On 22nd April a new fighter station was officially opened at Debden, about three miles to the south-east of Saffron Walden alongside the A130 road. It is said that the site of this new station was first recognised when a Bristol Bulldog had made an emergency landing back in May 1935. Debden's first Station Commander was Wing Commander S.L.G. Pope, D.F.C., A.F.C., and it was planned to be a three-squadron station. The first squadron, No 87, arrived on 7th June; it had reformed at Tangmere in March with Hawker Furies but, after their arrival at Debden, the pilots received their new fighters, Gloster Gladiators. A few days later 73 Squadron moved in from Mildenhall with its Furies.

The Gladiator had first flown in September 1934 and had undergone Service trials in the following March but did not begin to enter the R.A.F. until February 1937. It was the first fighter to be provided with an enclosed cockpit but also proved to be the last of the Service's biplane fighters. Without doubt, the Gladiator was a superb fighter, perhaps the ultimate in biplane design; all its pilots agreed that it was 'a sheer delight to fly'. It had a top speed of 250 m.p.h. and was armed with four .303 machine guns. However, with so many Hurricanes and Spitfires on order and the Air Ministry's long delay in ordering the Gladiator, it was virtually obsolete when entering the Service. Nevertheless production continued and by the outbreak of war the R.A.F. had over 300 Gladiators and a handful of them memorably and gallantly fought in the defence of Malta.

The other three squadrons in Essex also converted to Gladiators during the year.

In the summer, Southend Airport (or Rochford as it was always named in R.A.F. records) was used as a summer camp for three Auxiliary Air Force squadrons – 601 (County of London), 602 (City of Glasgow) and 607 (County of Durham); 602 Squadron flew Hawker Hinds whereas the other two squadrons were equipped with Demons. No 602 (City of Glasgow) Squadron was formally presented with its official badge by Air Commodore Gable, C.B.E., D.S.O., whilst at Rochford. The badge bore a red lion rampant on a blue saltire, which recognised its Scottish origins, and the motto – *Cave Leonem Cruciatam* – translates to 'Beware the tormented beast'. Another part of Essex was also used for a R.A.F. summer camp. Fridaywood Farm, not far from the old wartime landing ground at Blackheath Common, Colchester, was used by Hawker Hectors of No 2 (Army Co-operation) Squadron.

There was more than a touch of irony when, on 23rd October, R.A.F. Hornchurch was officially visited by two *Luftwaffe* Generals, Erhard Milch and Ernst Udet, and Major Polte, the German Air Attaché in London. The renascent German Air Force, originally *Reichsluftwaffe,* officially came into being on 1st March 1935 and eight days later Adolf Hitler announced its existence to the world; in fact, Erhard Milch had been the leading architect in its rapid growth and development. The resurgent *Luftwaffe* was the main reason for the R.A.F.'s expansion programme.

The German officers had visited several other R.A.F. stations. The pilots were under strict orders not to show the new reflector gun sights that had recently been installed. The German officers were probably not too concerned with what they saw at Hornchurch – all biplane fighters – especially as their Messerschmitt Bf 109, a far faster monoplane fighter, was already in action with the Condor Legion in the Spanish Civil War.

On 11th November 1937, the affairs of the Aero 8 Club were wound up, which effectively marked the end of Canute Air Park, and on the same day Messrs Chadwick and Gordon registered Romford Flying Club Ltd as a private company with capital of £500. It acquired the interests and property of the old club at Maylands and the new club's managing director was 'Captain' Raymond Gordon, as he now appeared to be known, with Mervyn Chadwick as director. At least now, albeit for a rather brief period, Maylands aerodrome came back to life.

Chapter 13

The Gathering Storm (1938–September 1939)

During 1938 the worsening political situation in Europe cast ever lengthening and darkening shadows over aviation in the country, be it civil, club or private, and it was almost impossible to escape from news of military flying and the seemingly endless talk of an approaching war. It is not surprising therefore that the Royal Air Force virtually dominated the aviation scheme in Essex during these last twenty months of peace.

Recruitment for the R.A.F. Volunteer Reserve had begun in earnest in April 1937 with the intention of producing 800 pilots each year but the response had been far beyond the Air Ministry's wildest expectations. The existing nine Elementary & Reserve Flying Training Schools, which were civilian flying schools under contract to the Air Ministry, were unable to cope with the number of volunteers and another twenty were formed during 1938.

No 21 E. & R.F.T.S. was established at Stapleford aerodrome by Reid & Sigrist Ltd, which started its flying training on 1 January equipped mainly with de Havilland Tiger Moths along with some

R.A.F.V.R. student pilots received flying training at Stapleford aerodrome and Southend Airport.

Hawker Hart trainers. Without doubt the most famous pupil to receive his flying training at Stapleford was J.E. 'Johnnie' Johnson, who was then a civil engineer at Loughton. Johnson became the R.A.F.'s top-scoring pilot with 38 victories. He later recalled his flying instructor's warning about Hurricanes from nearby North Weald: 'Keep a sharp look-out for those brutes. They come at you at a terrific speed and, head on, look no bigger than a razor blade'! Towards the end of the year another School was formed at Southend Airport when No 34 was established by Air Hire Ltd. By 1st September 1939 the R.A.F.V.R.'s aircrew strength was over 10,200, of which some 6,400 were pilots.

Hurricanes had entered the Service the previous December to be the R.A.F.'s first monoplane fighter. They made headline news on

10th February when Squadron Leader J.W. Gillan, the Commander of No 111 Squadron, flew from Edinburgh to Northolt, a distance of 327 miles, in 48 minutes. Even allowing for a strong tail-wind this was a remarkable performance, demonstrating that the aircraft truly lived up to its name.

The first Hurricanes appeared at North Weald in May 1938 with No 56, the third squadron to convert to them. They were powered by Rolls-Royce Merlin II engines and were capable of a top speed of 330 m.p.h., armed with eight .303 machine guns. The Hurricane was a sturdy and reliable aircraft, highly manoeuvrable, able to withstand considerable damage and its pilots accounted for more enemy aircraft in the Battle of Britain than its more illustrious rival, the Spitfire. The 'Hurry', as it was fondly called, inspired great loyalty in its pilots. By the end of 1938 two hundred Hurricanes were serving in various squadrons, 85 and 87 at Debden and, in December, 151 Squadron began exchanging its Gauntlets for Hurricanes. The arrival of these remarkable fighters at a fighter station also brought a couple of Fairey Battles and Miles Magisters, which were used to train the pilots on conversion to monoplanes.

Empire Air Day held on 28th May attracted larger crowds than usual and perhaps the heavy rain discouraged even greater numbers from attending. Nevertheless over 10,000 turned up at Hornchurch and they were able to witness a fly-past of Hurricanes from North Weald and also to see the latest celebrated woman pilot, New Zealander Jean Batten; she arrived in her Percival Gull Six which, during the previous October, she had flown from Australia in five days and eighteen hours, close to the existing record.

The 'petticoat pilots' were at long last getting some due recognition. In May the Air Ministry asked the Women's Legion to recruit women pilots who might be useful to the R.A.F. in the time of war. Then there were over 210 women pilots out of a total of some 4,500 'A' licensed pilots. As the *Evening Standard* commented: 'This is the first recognition given since 1918 to any part which women may be able to play in air defence'. This

Hurricanes of No 56 Squadron – 'Keep a sharp look-out for those brutes. They come at you at a terrific speed…'.

initiative led to the formation of the National Women's Air Reserve and ultimately to the Women's Section of the Air Transport Auxiliary.

On 9th July, Pauline Gower was one of a number of women pilots attending a rally of the National Women's Air Reserve held at Maylands aerodrome; it was billed as 'The Great Women's Air Rally'. Unfortunately heavy cloud and rain prevented much flying but Pauline Gower and Miss Joan Everard performed what was advertised as 'strip-tease bombing'; according to a report in *The Aeroplane*, 'the two ladies dressed in Victorian clothes flew low over a car and bombarded it with bags of flour, on each occasion feminine garments of ever increasing intimacy were also thrown out of the aeroplane…when they landed, a figure in nightdress shot out from the front cockpit and raced for cover with Charley's Auntish trouser legs showing below the skirt.' Despite the poor weather over 60 passengers were taken on joy-rides. This rally proved to be the last formal air display to take place in Essex before the outbreak of war.

An exciting and innovative scheme, the Civil Air Guard (C.A.G.), was announced on 23rd July 1938 by Sir Kingsley Wood, the

Another celebrated woman pilot, Jean Batten; she attended the Empire Air Day at Hornchurch on 28th May 1938.

Secretary of State for Air, as part of the National Defence Programme. The Scheme was open to 'healthy applicants of either sex between the ages of 18 and 50 years'. They would receive heavily subsidised flying training, providing they agreed to serve in 'any capacity at a time of national emergency'. It was proposed to commence the Scheme on 1st September and the flying training would be undertaken, purely on a volunteer basis, by the 62 private flying clubs around the country. Those clubs prepared to enter the Scheme were required to obtain at least twelve members to form a 'Unit' and in return they would receive a £50 payment for each successful member obtaining an 'A' licence. The flying tuition charges were restricted to ten shillings per hour at weekends and five shillings on weekdays.

There was a remarkable response to the C.A.G.; some 35,000 applications were received in the first three months, 6,000 were immediately accepted and enrolled and the rest were placed on long waiting lists. An initial fee of £14 was charged to the new members, which included the provision of helmet, goggles, flying suit and membership of the Royal Aero Club. It was estimated that for about £10 for flying lessons most would obtain their coveted licence, when they would be issued with a small C.A.G. lapel badge

Pauline Gower's Spartan three-seater was often seen in Essex.

with wings. The Marquess of Londonderry was appointed Chief Commissioner of the C.A.G. and Mrs Maxine Miles, the wife of F.G. Miles, the aircraft manufacturer, as the Woman Commissioner. By May 1939 over 2,000 members had obtained their licences and had actually been classified in categories 'relating to their prospective value at a time of war'! Some served in the R.A.F. but many were recruited to the A.T.A. and ferried aircraft from factories and reserve stores to operational stations.

Both Southend and Romford Flying Clubs entered the scheme. Unlike the E. & R.F.T. Schools there was no restriction on the type of aircraft used for flying training and thus a wide variety of trainers was used, although mainly D.H 94 Moth Minors, Miles M.14 Hawk Trainers and B.A. Swallow 11s. However, Southend Flying Club had purchased two Czech-built Zin monoplane trainers from Essex Aero Ltd at Gravesend, which had acquired the British agency for these foreign aircraft.

Maylands aerodrome was no longer considered safe for flying training because of the rapid build-up of housing around Harold Wood. The Flying Club was forced to find a more suitable site and

This publicity photograph of Civil Air Guard trainees was probably taken at Chigwell aerodrome.

as a result a small aerodrome at Chigwell was brought into use. It was located to the north-east of the junction of Hainault Road and Forest Farm, about a mile or so from the old Forest Farm landing ground. On 24th September the aerodrome was officially opened by Mrs Maxine Miles, who was universally known as 'Blossom'. She appropriately arrived in one of her husband's M.17 Monarchs, G–AFLW, a rather splendid cabin monoplane and the last light aircraft built in Britain for the private market before the war. She was accompanied by Pauline Gower in her Spartan three-seater, G–ACAD, which was frequently seen at Southend and Chigwell after Miss Gower became the C.A.G. Commissioner for the South-East in May 1939.

In its short existence Chigwell aerodrome featured twice in aviation journals. An article on the Civil Air Guard that appeared in *The Aeroplane* also carried a photograph with the caption: 'Keen to get to the controls, enthusiastic girl members of the C.A.G. rush to their machines in Chingford (Essex)'. As there was then no

Bristol Bombay: the prototype – K3583 – landed at Chigwell aerodrome on 4th February 1939.

aerodrome at Chingford the photograph must have been taken at Chigwell.

In February 1939 there was a report that a large prototype aircraft made an emergency forced landing at Chigwell on the 4th. Whilst attempting to take off the undercarriage had collapsed and the aircraft was damaged beyond repair. This aircraft was a Bristol Type 130 or Bombay, K3583, which was a large long-range troop or cargo carrier that had first flown in June 1935. The first production Bombays did not appear until March 1939 and finally entered the R.A.F. in September 1939. Considering that the longest landing strip at Chigwell was 2,400 ft it is quite remarkable that this massive high-wing twin-engine monoplane was able to land there; with a wingspan of nearly 96 ft and a length of over 63 ft it was, to the best of my knowledge, the largest aircraft to land in Essex during the pre-war years.

Since the days of Handley Page this corner of Essex had attracted several landing grounds and aerodromes and in the late 1930s the City of London Corporation had purchased an area of land to the south side of Forest Road, which was known as Fairlop Plain. The Corporation had plans to build a City of London airport but, because of the unsettled political situation, its development was placed on hold. Shortly after the outbreak of the war the land was

Hurricanes of No 151 Squadron take off from North Weald. (Imperial War Museum)

acquired by the Air Ministry and developed into a fighter station, which opened on 1st August 1941 as R.A.F. Fairlop.

In 1938 the old aerodrome at Clacton-on-Sea was taken over by the Straight Corporation with plans to improve the landing field and the facilities. The company had been founded in April 1935 by Whitney Straight, a wealthy American former racing driver, and over the next few years he acquired several aerodromes (notably Ipswich and Exeter), a number of flying clubs and even an airline, Southern Airways. Although Clacton aerodrome was not developed to the same extent as the other aerodromes, a passenger service was started between Clacton-on-Sea and Ipswich, operated by a Short Scion. There were also ample opportunities for pleasure flights from Clacton.

Formation of No 65 Squadron's Spitfires in August 1939. Their code was changed to 'YT' in September.

The Air Ministry decided to put down two permanent concrete runways at North Weald; one was 933 yds long and the other 923 yds and each 50 ft wide. This was unique for a fighter station in those days, although Air Marshal Sir Hugh Dowding maintained at the time that, 'we must have these runways at almost all fighter stations if we are to be able to operate fighters by day and night during a wet winter'. Another reason may have been the heavier fighters that were coming into the Service – for instance, the Hurricane's maximum take-off weight was three-and-a-quarter tons compared with the Gladiator at some two tons.

Shortly after the annual Home Defence Air Exercises in August all three fighter stations were placed on a full war alert as a result of what is now known as the 'Munich crisis'. For most of September 1938 the country seemed to be on the brink of war with Germany. All personnel on leave were recalled, Operations Rooms were manned on a 24-hour basis, squadrons were placed on 30-minute readiness and, for the first time, all their fighters were camouflaged, much to ground

The first Bristol Blenheim Ifs to appear in Essex arrived at North Weald on 2nd September 1939.

crews' and pilots' disgust; the gleaming aircraft resplendent in their squadron markings were painted a dull green and brown. This emergency was a taste of what was to come in less than twelve months. The whole country breathed a huge sigh of relief when the Prime Minister, Neville Chamberlain, returned to Heston Airport on 30th September after signing the Munich Agreement.

On 19th October, North Weald was the location for an unique event when, according to a R.A.F. Intelligence Bulletin, 'the British Broadcasting Co-operation [sic] included in their normal television programme a live outside television broadcast of Hurricanes of 56 and 151 Squadrons carrying out formation flying over North Weald, affording the public the first opportunity to view the Service's aircraft in training'. Just how many (or how few?) were actually able to witness this live transmission is debatable because in 1936 it was estimated that fewer than 20,000 households in the country owned a television set!

A most auspicious day for Hornchurch was on 13th February 1939 when the first Supermarine Spitfire, K9860, arrived for No 74

Squadron. It had been flown from the Supermarine factory at Eastleigh by Squadron Leader D.S. Brookes, who had previously commanded the squadron. No 54's first Spitfire arrived on 3rd March and 65 Squadron was the last to receive their new fighters on 21st March.

Without doubt, the Spitfire was the most famous Allied fighter of the Second World War and first entered the R.A.F. with 19 Squadron at Duxford during August 1938. With a top speed of close to 360 m.p.h., it was thought to be the fastest fighter in the world and like the Hurricane it was armed with eight .303 machine guns, making it a most formidable fighter. Pilots were universal in their praise: '[it] had style and was an obvious killer...she was a perfect lady. She had no vices, it was the most beautiful flying machine ever invented'. Even today the sound and sight of a Spitfire evokes tremendous excitement. Hornchurch with its three Spitfire squadrons was unique in Fighter Command.

The sixth and final Empire Air Day was celebrated on 20th May and over one million people attended the sixty-three Service airfields and fifteen civil aerodromes that were opened throughout the country. Most felt that this was likely to be the last occasion to see the R.A.F. at close quarters. Almost 45,000 people crowded into Hornchurch, no doubt attracted by the thought of seeing the much publicised new and exciting fighter; they also saw Alex Henshaw, a well-known racing pilot, arrive in his Percival Mew Gull. During the war, as Chief Test Pilot for Vickers-Supermarine, Henshaw probably flew more Spitfires than any other airman.

A total of over 15,000 people entered North Weald's gates for the last time; it too was a record attendance for the Station. Three days later 17 Squadron's Gauntlets arrived at North Weald from Kenley to bring its complement back to three squadrons. However, the squadron stayed for about two-and-a-half months during which time its pilots converted to Hurricanes before returning to Kenley. Just a week after the outbreak of war 17 Squadron moved to Debden.

As it seemed abundantly clear that the country was on the brink of war with Germany, the Home Defence Air Exercises that took place from 8th to 11th August were the largest ever mounted and the most significant. Over 1,300 aircraft were involved along with the Radio Direction Finding (Radar) stations, anti-aircraft and searchlight batteries and barrage balloons. A new radio location signal was trialled for the first time. This was a signal transmitted by 'friendly' aircraft, which could be recognised by ground operators; it later became known as I.F.F. for 'Identification Friend or Foe'. On the 11th, 54's Spitfires were sent to Southend Airport to patrol over the North Sea. In the evening of 12th August Air Chief Marshal Sir Hugh Dowding made a BBC broadcast to assure the public of its safety from air attack: 'I confidently believe that serious attack on these Islands would be brought to a standstill within a short space of time'.

Ten days later the R.A.F. was effectively placed on a war footing. Fighter squadrons were placed on a 30-minute readiness and the aircraft were dispersed around the perimeters of airfields, with tents for duty pilots placed within 25 yards of their aircraft. All leave was cancelled and regular personnel were recalled from leave. The only flights allowed were emergency air tests. On the 27th, members of the Volunteer Reserve were called up. With effect from midnight on 31st August the Air Navigation (Emergency Restriction) Order prohibited any flights by civil and private aircraft over the eastern half of the country.

On 2nd September 1939 a General Mobilisation of the R.A.F. was ordered, to include the Auxiliary Air Force and Reserves. No 604 (County of Middlesex) Squadron, equipped with Bristol Blenheim 1Fs, arrived at North Weald to bring the station up to its full complement of squadrons. On Sunday, 3rd September the signal went out from 11 and 12 Groups to all their fighter stations: 'War has broken out with Germany only'.

The pilots of the nine fighter squadrons then based in Essex – 54, 65 and 74 at Hornchurch; 56, 151 and 604 at North Weald; and 29, 85 and 87 at Debden – were ready and eager to meet the

Luftwaffe. Over the next six years young airmen of many nationalities would fly a wide range of bombers and fighters from the 23 wartime airfields located in the county. They would bravely forge a most memorable and glorious chapter in the aviation heritage and history of Essex.

Bibliography

Baker, W. J., *A History of Marconi Company* (Methuen, 1970)

Barfoot, John, *Over Here and Over There: Ilford Aerodromes and Airmen in the Great War* (Ian Henry Publications, 1998)

Barfoot, John, *Essex Airmen 1910–1918* (Tempus Publishing Ltd, 2006)

Bruce, Mildred, *Nine Lives Plus: Record Breaking on Land, Sea and in the Air* (Pelham Books, 1977)

Butler, Nicholas, *The Story of Wivenhoe* (Quentin Press, 1989)

Castle, H. E., *Fire Over England: the German Air Raids in WWI* (Secker & Warburg, 1982)

Cole, K. A. (editor*)*, *A History of Aviation in Essex* (Southend Branch of the Royal Aeronautical Society, 1967)

Cruddas, Colin, *Those Fabulous Flying Years* (Air Britain (Historians), 2003)

de Havilland, Geoffrey, *Sky Fever* (Airlife Publications, 1979)

Dowsett, Paul A., *Fields of the First: A History of Landing Grounds used during the First World War* (Forward Airfield Research Publications, 1997)

Goodall, Michael & Tagg, Albert E., *British Aircraft before the Great War* (Schiffer Aviation History Book, 2001)

Hyde, Andrew P., *The First Blitz: the German Air Campaign against Britain, 1917–18* (Leo Cooper, 2002)

Jackson, A. J., *Avro Aircraft since 1908* (Putnam, 1965)

Jarrett, P. (editor), *Early Aviation before 1914* (Putnam Aeronautical Books, 2002)

Lewis, Cecil A., *Sagittarius Rising* (Peter Davies, 1944)

Lewis, Cecil A., *Farewell to Wings* (Temple Books, 1964)

Munson, James (editor), *Echoes of the Great War: the Diary of the Reverend Andrew Clark, 1914–1919* (Oxford University Press, 1985)

Penrose, Harald J., *British Aviation: 1. The Pioneer Years, 1903–1914* (Cassell, 1967) *4. Widening Horizons, 1930–1934* (H.M.S.O., 1979)

Philpot, Anthony K., *Maylands Aerodrome: the Story of a Small Independent Airfield 1928–1940* (Ian Henry, 2003)

Poolman, Kenneth, *Zeppelins over England* (White Lion Publishers, 1975)

Rolt, L. T. C., The *Aeronauts: A History of Ballooning, 1783-1903*, (Longmans Green, 1966)

Smith, Eric, *'First Things First': R.A.F. Hornchurch, R.A.F. Suttons Farm, 1915–1962* (Ian Henry, 1992)

Smith, Graham, *Essex Airfields in the Second World War* (Countryside Books, 1996)

Smith, Graham, *Taking to the Skies: the Story of British Aviation, 1903–1939* (Countryside Books, 2003)

Smith, Richard C., *Hornchurch Scramble: Vol. 1. 1915 to the end of the Battle of Britain* (Grub Street, 2000)

Smith, Ron, *British Built Aircraft. Vol. 3. South-East England* (Tempus Publishing Ltd, 2004)

Stoney, Barbara, *Twentieth Century Maverick: the Life of Noel Pemberton Billing* (Bank House Books, 2004)

Wallace, Graham, *Claude Grahame-White* (Putnam, 1960)

Over the decades *Essex Countryside* has published a number of articles on early aviation in the county, some are listed below:

Baker, T.A., *Mr Churchill's Lost Weekend. The Best of Essex*, 1988.

Davies, Leonard, *Early Days of Flight at Chingford.* June, 1997.

Elliott, Bryn, *An Air Pioneer: brief life of aviator B.C. Hucks.* April, 1997.

Frost, K.A., *Gothas over Essex.* May, 1968.

Hunt, Leslie, *Sixty years of Flying in Essex.* April, 1968.

Possee, David, *Zeppelins over Braintree.* November, 1996.

Smith, Eric R., *Last Zeppelin over Essex.* July, 1997.

Index